"This workbook is a terrific resource for individuals dealing with social anxiety, as well as for therapists supporting them. Grounded in evidence-based practices, it is both accessible and highly practical. The workbook offers a clear, step-by-step approach to understanding the core elements of social anxiety, and provides actionable strategies for overcoming it. With a thoughtful blend of insightful instruction, engaging exercises, and helpful examples, this guide is an invaluable tool. I highly recommend it!"

—**Judith S. Beck, PhD**, president of the Beck Institute for Cognitive Behavior Therapy, and author of *Cognitive Behavior Therapy: Basics and Beyond* and *Cognitive Therapy for Challenging Problems*

"A strongly recommended read for anyone whose life is held back by social anxiety disorder (SAD). Larry Cohen draws on a wealth of clinical experience to elegantly outline many of the most effective techniques in cognitive behavioral therapy (CBT), with particular focus on the feelings of shame that accompany much of social anxiety."

—**David M. Clark, DPhil**, emeritus professor of psychology at the University of Oxford

"Is shyness and social anxiety holding you back? Are you missing out in life and feeling trapped because of it? This book will open the doors to a better, more meaningful, and happier life. Larry Cohen has created an excellent, well-written, and hands-on book that will guide you on your journey to break free from the chains of social anxiety and shyness. Don't wait and suffer in silence. Use this book. It will change your life."

—**Stefan G. Hofmann, PhD**, professor of psychology at Philipps-University Marburg, Germany; and author of *CBT for Social Anxiety*

"Larry has made a game-changing contribution to self-therapy for social anxiety. Using years of clinical experience treating socially anxious clients and a deep knowledge of cutting-edge social anxiety treatment research, Larry developed a comprehensive program integrating common approaches to social anxiety treatment. The well-described exercises will help users make ongoing social interactions and performance changes."

—**John R. Montopoli, LMFT, LPCC, A-CBT**, cofounder of the National Social Anxiety Center (NSAC), and director of Pacific Cognitive Behavioral Therapy

"This is a carefully constructed and elegant self-help resource. Larry takes our wealth of knowledge about social anxiety and breaks it down into a series of innovative and easy-to-understand steps bolstered with carefully designed practice forms. Third-wave CBT strategies are incorporated into his approach to provide additional tools to overcome social anxiety. As a pioneer in treating social anxiety, Larry infuses wisdom and empathy from his experience into this workbook."

—**Vince Greenwood, PhD,** executive director of the Washington Center for Cognitive Therapy, and founder of www.dutytoinform.org

"Larry Cohen has years of experience helping people with social anxiety. In this book, his experience shines through. Larry's empathy and understanding bring alive the life-changing guidelines that he describes. And let's be clear—this book will change your life. It takes scientifically proven methods to treat social anxiety that are explained through Larry's clear, easy-to-follow style. If your life is affected by social fears, this book is for you."

—**Ronald M. Rapee, PhD, AM,** distinguished professor of psychology at Macquarie University, and author of *Helping Your Anxious Child*

"This terrific workbook will be a boon for anyone seeking to move through the world with greater comfort and confidence. The core idea that social anxiety typically results from feelings of shame about oneself is, in my experience, exactly right. The book draws on the latest research and clinical innovations to provide the reader with practical tools to help overcome social anxiety. This is a book I will be recommending to my patients."

—**Stephen J. F. Holland, PsyD,** director of the Capital Institute for Cognitive Therapy, and author of *Treatment Plans and Interventions for Depression and Anxiety Disorders*

Overcoming Shame-Based Social Anxiety & Shyness

A CBT Workbook to Move Past Feelings of Self-Consciousness or Defectiveness & Live with Confidence

LARRY COHEN, LICSW, A-CBT

New Harbinger Publications, Inc.

Publisher's Note

This publication is designed to provide accurate and authoritative information in regard to the subject matter covered. It is sold with the understanding that the publisher is not engaged in rendering psychological, financial, legal, or other professional services. If expert assistance or counseling is needed, the services of a competent professional should be sought.

NEW HARBINGER PUBLICATIONS is a registered trademark of New Harbinger Publications, Inc.

New Harbinger Publications is an employee-owned company.

Copyright © 2025 by Larry Cohen
New Harbinger Publications, Inc.
5720 Shattuck Avenue
Oakland, CA 94609
www.newharbinger.com

All Rights Reserved

Cover design by Amy Shoup

Acquired by Wendy Millstine and Jess O'Brien

Edited by Rona Bernstein

Library of Congress Cataloging-in-Publication Data on file

Printed in the United States of America

27 26 25

10 9 8 7 6 5 4 3 2 1   First Printing

Contents

	Foreword	V
	Introduction	1
CHAPTER 1	The Vicious Cycle of Social Anxiety and Shame	5
CHAPTER 2	Identifying Your Own Vicious Cycles	13
CHAPTER 3	External Mindfulness: Getting Out of Your Head and into the Moment	27
CHAPTER 4	Behavioral Experiments: Testing Your Anxious Hot Thoughts and Shame-Based Core Beliefs	37
CHAPTER 5	Being a Good Parent to Yourself: Counteracting Self-Critical Rumination	49
CHAPTER 6	Reframing: Making Your Thoughts Realistic, Helpful, and Compassionate	57
CHAPTER 7	Confident Imagery: Using Your Imagination to Change Your Thinking	69
CHAPTER 8	Pride and Gratitude: Defeating Your Negativity Bias	75
CHAPTER 9	Paradoxical Experiments: Confronting Your Anxiety and Shame	83
CHAPTER 10	Head-Held-High Assertion: Standing Up for Yourself	91
CHAPTER 11	Going Deeper: Identifying and Changing Your Shame-Based Core Beliefs	105
CHAPTER 12	Rebelling and Acting as if: Using Experiments to Change Your Core Beliefs	117
CHAPTER 13	That Was Then, This Is Now: Learning to Let Go of the Past	131
CHAPTER 14	Continuing Forward: Making Progress on Your Own	147
	References	161

Foreword

If you have picked up this book, you are probably aware that social anxiety disorder can be a big problem, one that can disrupt your life in numerous ways. You have probably felt its effects in several areas of your life, such as in your relationships with others, or your work or school performance. You may have felt discouraged or even hopeless about the possibility of a future without the weight of social anxiety on your shoulders. However, there is very good reason to take a more optimistic view. There is substantial scientific evidence that cognitive behavioral therapy (CBT)—a form of psychological therapy that involves changing the ways you think and behave in order to change the way you feel—can produce meaningful and lasting improvements in one's social anxiety. Change is never easy, but CBT provides a systematic approach that has benefitted many thousands of people the world over.

Larry Cohen should know. Larry is a highly experienced clinician who, since 1990, has provided CBT to an untold number of clients with social anxiety disorder through his practice, Social Anxiety Help, in Washington, DC. In 2014, he cofounded the National Social Anxiety Center (NSAC), an association of independent clinics (now more than 30!) staffed by cognitive behavioral therapists specializing in the treatment of social anxiety that also provides information, education, and training related to social anxiety. Through his work with the NSAC, Larry has probably made treatment for social anxiety more visible and more accessible to more people in the United States than any other clinician. He knows a thing or two about social anxiety and how to address it.

In this workbook, Larry presents an integrationist approach to CBT for social anxiety. He has taken the best from the work of leading clinical scientists (e.g., David M. Clark, Stefan Hofmann, Ronald Rapee, myself) and master clinicians (e.g., Christine Padesky), combined with his own extensive clinical experience, and presents it to you in a step-by-step form that you can apply in your day-to-day to begin to take back your life from the grips of social anxiety disorder.

Larry leads you on a journey of self-discovery that teaches you to take the approach of a compassionate clinical scientist to understanding and working with your social anxiety. As a person with social anxiety, you likely have negative thoughts about your performance in various social situations and about your worth as a person. You may even feel intense shame, which can make it very difficult to pay attention to what is going on around you. You may have very high expectations for yourself in these situations and count yourself a failure if you fail to meet them. Larry will teach you to identify these thoughts and beliefs you have about yourself and how to challenge them in a kind and compassionate way. Imagine for a moment how different life would be if you could treat yourself with the kindness and compassion that you would offer a child in distress!

Larry provides many techniques and strategies to help you come to that kinder and more compassionate place. I highlight a couple of them here. One key strategy is to approach social situations as a scientist would approach an experiment. In a "behavioral experiment," you select a social situation you wish to work on and make a hypothesis about how it will turn out. The situation might be a conversation with a casual acquaintance at a party, and the hypothesis might be your negative prediction about how the situation would turn out (e.g., that you won't have anything to say). You also set some goals for your behavior in the situation, such as to initiate at least one topic of conversation, and you see how it goes—that is, you look to the data of what really happened rather than the predictions of gloom and doom that may have prevented you from trying this out in the first place. Behavioral experiments can be very powerful in helping you reshape your thoughts and beliefs about yourself. If this sounds a bit scary, start with easier situations before moving on to more difficult ones.

Another key strategy is something Larry refers to as external mindfulness, which is focusing your attention outward on the situation rather than inward on your negative thoughts and worries. In the situation of talking to a casual acquaintance at a party, it's important to focus your attention on the other person rather than yourself, and to do so with a sense of genuine curiosity or interest in what the other person is saying rather than a sense of evaluation or judgment.

There are many more techniques and strategies that Larry will lead you through. They are not easy! In fact, they are likely to temporarily cause you some anxiety if you choose to give them a try. So go slow, try things out multiple times, and don't let perfect be the enemy of good. Your hard work will be amply rewarded!

Good luck on your journey.

—Richard G. Heimberg, PhD
Thaddeus A. Bolton Professor of Psychology
and Neuroscience Emeritus
Temple University

Introduction

Social anxiety disorder is very common, painfully life restricting and, without proper treatment, usually lifelong (National Institute of Mental Health [NIMH] 2024; Bruce et al. 2005). The good news is that evidence-based treatments are available that help the large majority of those struggling with social anxiety disorder—or more broadly, shyness—overcome these problems and lead fuller, more satisfying lives. This workbook presents a self-led approach to the most effective of these treatments: cognitive behavioral therapy, or CBT (Mayo-Wilson et al. 2014).

Most self-help books about social anxiety and shyness—and many therapist manuals, as well—focus almost entirely on helping people overcome the severe impact that anxiety has had on their lives. And this restricted approach is usually greatly beneficial. But, for the large majority of sufferers, social anxiety, often called social phobia, is more than a simple phobia: an exaggerated and life-restricting fear. Unlike all other phobias, *social anxiety is based on shame-generating core beliefs about fundamental personal deficiency and perfectionistic self-expectations, which in turn lead to the exaggerated fear of judgment and rejection that is the hallmark of social anxiety and shyness.* Shame is, for most people, a key ingredient in their social anxiety or shyness.

This CBT workbook guides you step by step through an in-depth, comprehensive self-therapy program that addresses both the anxiety and the shame that constitute your social anxiety and shyness. I have used these CBT strategies since 1990 in helping more than 1,000 people overcome their social anxiety and shame. I cofounded and have led the National Social Anxiety Center (NSAC) since 2014: a network of dozens of CBT clinics around the US that have expertise in helping people overcome social anxiety. And I've trained hundreds of psychotherapists around the country to enable them to provide effective, evidenced-based therapy for people suffering from social anxiety and shame. I consider it a privilege to enable you to benefit from these same strategies.

Which of the following situations and interactions trigger in you a high level of anxiety (fear that something bad will happen) or shame (feeling bad about yourself as a person)? Check and circle those that apply:

- ☐ Meeting people and interacting with strangers
- ☐ Socializing
- ☐ Making conversation

- ☐ Making new friends and pursuing current friendships
- ☐ Dating and pursuing romantic relationships
- ☐ Speaking in or presenting to groups
- ☐ Asserting your opinions or feelings
- ☐ Doing things when you may be observed by others (e.g., sports, talking on the phone, writing, eating, shopping, working, dancing, stage performing, using public bathrooms, being sexual)

It's normal and sometimes even helpful to feel a bit nervous and hesitant in any of these situations. But if your anxiety causes you a great deal of distress or shame, leads you to avoid or hold back too much, hurts your conversation or performance, or results in self-consciousness, self-criticism, worry, or other rumination, then this self-therapy program is designed for you.

In addition to addressing both shame and anxiety, this workbook stands out by being an integrative CBT approach to social anxiety, bringing together the evidence-based strategies from all three "waves" of cognitive behavioral therapy. From first-wave (behaviorally focused) CBT, we incorporate exposure therapy while eliminating your unhelpful safety-seeking behaviors and building confidence in your social skills. From second-wave (cognitively focused) CBT, we utilize behavioral experiments designed to test and change anxious "hot thoughts" and shame-based core beliefs, as well as strategies to reframe your thinking to lessen anxiety and enhance pride. Second-wave CBT has been demonstrated to be the most effective treatment for social anxiety (Mayo-Wilson et al. 2014). From third-wave (mindfulness-based) CBT—including acceptance and commitment therapy, or ACT—we incorporate strategies to focus externally and mindfully on doing activities you value when your anxiety or shame is triggered.

Additionally, numerous free tools are available for you to access on the website for this book, http://www.newharbinger.com/54322. The free tools are organized into four documents: Guide to the Online Free Tools, Resources, Worksheets, and Bonus Chapter Supplements. All of the worksheets mentioned in the book are contained in the free tools for you to download. Throughout this book, this icon alerts you to specific free tools available to help you put into effect what is being described in that passage.

To benefit the most from this workbook, keep in mind the following tips:

1. **Do the in-chapter exercises and the between-chapter homework.** This is a *self-therapy workbook*. It's designed to guide you, step by step, to learn and *practice* many cognitive (i.e., thought-related) and behavioral strategies and skills to help you overcome social anxiety and shame. Every chapter after the first ends with suggestions for self-therapy homework for you to practice in the coming week(s), and each subsequent chapter begins with reviewing what you learned from the previous week's homework.

   Simply *reading* this book without practicing the exercises and homework will likely result in lots of learning…and minimal actual change in your life. The skills and strategies taught in this program are meant to serve you throughout your life. But skills and strategies take practice to master! This practice will lead to decreased anxiety and shame, increased self-confidence and pride, and progress toward the self-therapy goals you choose in chapter 1 (e.g., making friends, dating, advancing your career, public speaking, being assertive, using public bathrooms).

2. **Go slowly! There's no rush!** This self-therapy program is designed to help you develop new strategies and skills to overcome the social anxiety and shame that have oppressed you for much of your life. When mastered, these strategies and skills will benefit you throughout the rest of your life. Take the time to systematically and repeatedly practice what this program suggests. This way you'll internalize these strategies and skills as part of the way you live, and you won't forget about them after you put the book away. Spend a week or two between each chapter working on the suggested self-therapy homework practice before moving on to the next chapter. At this rate, it'll take you about four months to complete this program, well worth the investment in time and effort to experience the benefits you'll reap!

3. **Get support, if possible.** You can certainly pursue this self-therapy program strictly on your own. It takes a little courage—you'll be facing your fears in small steps that you choose—and a lot of perseverance—you'll need to take a great many small steps over the coming four months or so to overcome your social anxiety and shame. But it'll be easier and possibly more effective if you have support throughout this process. If you're already working with a therapist or counselor, ask them if you can discuss the work you're doing in this self-therapy program during your appointments. That therapist or counselor may even want to read the book as you do in order to be able to provide you with more active support and guidance. But even if you just spend ten minutes or so of your weekly sessions discussing the homework you're doing and what you're learning from it, you'll likely find that quite beneficial in keeping up your motivation and enhancing your progress.

Don't have a therapist or counselor? Perhaps you have a shy friend who might be open to working through this self-therapy program together with you. Or look in http://www.meetup.com and other online listings for support or social groups for shyness and social anxiety, which are quite common. Then ask them—either through online messaging or at in-person gatherings—if anyone would like to work together doing this self-therapy program. You'll likely have takers. Or start your own meetup group through this site for the purpose of working this program together. Whether with a friend or support group members, you can meet every week or two, in person or by video chat, to discuss the self-therapy homework each of you is doing chapter by chapter, provide support and encouragement to each other, and enhance everyone's learning. You may even choose to do some of the homework exercises together.

But don't be discouraged if you don't have support and need to pursue this self-therapy program on your own. You can make just as much progress individually so long as you take it slowly and do all the in-chapter exercises and between-chapter homework practice.

4. **Beware of perfectionism!** Striving to make progress and excel is a good quality that can help you move forward in life. But applying perfectionistic, all-or-nothing self-standards—judging yourself and your efforts as deficient because you didn't fulfill your expectations completely—results in discouragement and shame, lessens your motivation, and diminishes your progress. Perfectionism is part of why you're socially anxious in the first place! Pat yourself on the back for each positive step you take throughout this program, rather than beating yourself up for every imperfection—as this will help you feel better and make more progress.

You're about to embark on an important journey that can help you overcome the anxiety and shame that has oppressed you and reshape your life going forward. Take it slowly. Persevere. Pat yourself on the back for each step you take forward. You'll be learning and mastering strategies and skills that can benefit you throughout your life. I wish you much pride and progress in this journey!

CHAPTER 1

The Vicious Cycle of Social Anxiety and Shame

Let's begin this self-therapy program by exploring how you unintentionally get caught up in a vicious cycle of thoughts, feelings, and behaviors that ends up making you feel anxiety and shame, and hurt how you come across and perform.

Components of the Vicious Cycle

The experience of social anxiety involves a vicious cycle fueled by **core beliefs** of fundamental personal deficiency and perfectionistic self-expectations. These beliefs generate **hot thoughts** about conversing or performing badly and appearing anxious or foolish in situations where you fear your deficiencies may be exposed. These thoughts generate much **anxiety**, leading you to rely on **safety-seeking behaviors** in an effort to avoid making a bad impression. Examples of safety-seeking behaviors include avoidance, self-monitoring your performance and appearance, scripting what to say, and trying to hide your anxiety. But these behaviors backfire and actually *hurt* how you come across, converse, or perform: an unintentional self-fulfilling prophesy. Because of your **negativity bias** (i.e., a safety-seeking behavior in which you mainly focus on what you think may be going badly during an interaction), you believe you made a much worse impression than you actually did, which leads you to engage in self-critical **rumination and worry** after the triggering situation and before the next one. This, in turn, causes you to feel **shame** and reinforces your core beliefs of personal deficiency and perfectionistic self-expectations (Ginat-Frolich et al. 2024). The figure on the following page illustrates this vicious cycle.

Vicious Cycle of Social Anxiety and Shame

CORE BELIEFS about yourself and how others perceive you:
- fundamental personal deficiency
- perfectionistic self-expectations

HOT THOUGHTS about specific situations:
- worry that you will appear and perform badly
- worry that others will judge you for this and react badly
- sometimes leads to extended rumination about these worries

ANXIETY

SAFETY-SEEKING BEHAVIORS:
- avoidance
- self-focused attention on: your anxious feelings and symptoms; self-critiquing your conversation/performance; scripting what to say next
- negativity bias: focusing on what you think may be going badly
- other efforts to hide anxiety and deficiencies in conversation/performance

IMPACT of safety-seeking behaviors:
- your conversation or performance is hurt through distraction
- you come across as distracted and perhaps uninterested
- others may respond to you less well as a consequence
- you don't learn that you can handle the situation well without relying on safety-seeking behaviors, and that others will usually react well to you

RUMINATION AND WORRY about:
- how badly you think you came across
- how you fear others are thinking about you
- what you think is wrong with you and your life (while disqualifying, ignoring, or not even noticing what went well [i.e., negativity bias])

SHAME and sometimes also hopelessness and depression

CORE BELIEFS are seemingly reinforced

Let's take a close look at two common examples of social anxiety to see how this vicious cycle plays out.

Mingling with Strangers

Let's say you're invited to a party by a friendly coworker, Jason. You have a personal goal to make more friends, so you think that this party could be an opportunity to begin doing so. But you're troubled by old **core beliefs**—seemingly supported by years of painful evidence—that (1) you're really bad at socializing and meeting new people and (2) if others see you appear anxious or screw up in the conversation, they'll be turned off and think that you're weird or uninteresting.

In the past, you've generally avoided social activities out of fear that your social deficiencies and anxiety would show, that others would react negatively to you, and that you would end up with feeling shame and depression. You're very tempted to rely on your old **safety-seeking behavior** of avoidance this time, too. You spend a lot of time **ruminating, worrying**, and trying to figure out what to do. You consider telling Jason that you already have other plans that day. You think that Jason was just being nice in inviting you and doesn't really care if you come.

You scold yourself with **shame**: *What's the matter with me that I feel so anxious about going to a party?! Other people enjoy going to parties. Maybe this time will be different.* So you go.

After spending a lot of time **worrying** about what to wear, when to arrive, and whether you should come up with a last-minute excuse to not attend, you finally arrive at the party. With much **anxiety**, you quietly knock on the door and wait with mounting anxiety for what feels like a long time. You knock again, this time louder. Somebody answers the door, but it's not someone you know. You manage to say that you're here for Jason's party, and that person lets you in but doesn't introduce herself. You're left standing just inside the door as you look around the large room and see that it's crowded with people standing in small groups and actively chatting. You criticize yourself for not arriving earlier when there would have been fewer people. You're trying to figure out what to do. You think about leaving, but you feel ashamed and criticize yourself for even thinking so.

You finally see Jason across the room, chatting and laughing away with people you don't know. You can't hear what they're saying. You're trying to decide what to do, but you're troubled and frozen by anxious **hot thoughts**: *Should I go up to them and say hi, or would they think I'm intruding and being rude? Do others notice me standing alone so long, and are they thinking that I'm weird and unfriendly?* Then, to your surprise, Jason happens to turn a little. His eyes meet yours. He smiles and laughs. He turns back and continues laughing and chatting with his friends, who briefly glance your way, and then turn back.

You feel a surge of embarrassment. You have the **hot thoughts** that you've already made a terrible impression with Jason and his friends, who are probably saying negative things about you. Your anxiety is increasing, and you're thinking of just turning around and leaving, but feel too much **shame** for even considering that option. So you stay, take a deep breath, walk up to Jason, and timidly say hi to him and his friends.

They seem friendly enough. They try to make conversation with you, but you rely on your old **safety-seeking behaviors** of answering their questions in just a few words in order to get the attention off of yourself. You focus attention on your own anxious feelings and physical symptoms: your voice, which you think sounds horribly shaky with nervousness; your hands, which seem so jittery; and the warmth you feel in your face, which you imagine appears beet red. You also desperately try to script in your mind what to say next, and only come up with questions, again to keep the attention off of you. You criticize yourself for coming across so awkwardly. You end up just standing there quietly while Jason and his friends continue chatting, now ignoring you.

At some point you excuse yourself to go to the bathroom, where you spend time **ruminating** in self-criticism and feeling **shame**. After a prolonged escape in the bathroom—where you start feeling **anxiety** that others will think you're weird for being there so long—you finally return to the party, grab a drink, and engage in other **safety-seeking behaviors** of standing off by the side, quickly averting eye contact with people, and looking at your phone a lot in order to appear busy.

The few times somebody does come up to try to talk to you, you rely on your other **safety-seeking behaviors**: speaking very briefly, focusing on your anxiety symptoms, and trying to script what to say next. Each conversation is just as awkward and brief as the previous one. Your negativity bias kicks in, making you unaware that at least one person seemed to enjoy talking with you, and may even have been flirting with you. But by looking away and speaking only briefly, you came across as uninterested.

You finally sneak out of the party—too **anxious and ashamed** to say goodbye to anyone—and go home. There, off and on for weeks, you **ruminate** about how badly you think came across, feeling engulfed in **shame** about yourself and despair about your future. Your negativity bias keeps you stuck in self-criticism while disqualifying or ignoring the positive aspects of your attending the party. At work, you avoid or minimize interaction with Jason as much as possible out of fear of facing a negative reaction from him.

Speaking to a Group

Let's say you're at a meeting at work. Because you have the **core belief** that you're fundamentally deficient at conversing in groups, and that others will judge you as weird and incompetent if they see you screw up or appear anxious in any way, you rely on the **safety-seeking behavior** of sitting silently and just listening to others speak in order to keep attention off yourself.

But then someone asks you a question and your **anxiety** surges. You now engage in the **safety-seeking behavior** of speaking very briefly, even though you have much more you could say, because you hate the attention, which you assume to be critical. You focus on your anxious symptoms in the hope that you can hide them from the examining eyes of others. When it's your turn to present something, you focus on your notes or slides, reading them word for word rather than speaking freely, while avoiding looking at the audience. Your negativity bias leads you to home in on someone who appears uninterested while not noticing others who look quite interested in what you're saying. After the gathering, you **ruminate** in harsh self-criticism off and on for days, leaving you feeling deep **shame**, and setting yourself up to experience even more **anxiety** the next time you need to speak up in a group.

Breaking the Vicious Cycle

It doesn't have to be this way! We can learn to break the vicious cycle and experience a positive, virtuous cycle instead. Imagine that you go to the party or speak at the group gathering with the core belief that you have strengths and weaknesses like everyone else, and that you don't have to appear or perform perfectly for people to enjoy talking with you and be interested in what you have to say. Instead of relying on your safety-seeking behaviors, you focus your attention externally on what people are saying in the moment, and on expressing what pops into your mind naturally, without scripting. Instead of ruminating in self-criticism stemming from negativity bias afterward, you pat yourself on your back for the positive things you did and the positive experiences you had. You accept as completely normal that not every interaction will go ideally and that not everyone will like you, seeing that as just an indication that everyone has different preferences, not that you are deficient. Instead of feeling shame, you feel pride, self-confidence, and hopefulness for the future. Instead of worrying how the next interaction will go, you look forward to it as an opportunity for enjoyment and to move your life forward.

Easier said than done, right? Yes, that's true! But this book will guide you in engaging a step-by-step program of evidence-based cognitive behavioral therapy (CBT) that will help you break the vicious cycle of social anxiety and shame that has kept you stuck for most of your life.

SAD Facts

Social anxiety disorder (SAD) exists when the fear of judgment (including criticism, rejection, scrutiny, and embarrassment) makes it extremely difficult to pursue one or more major life activities and goals that are important to you, such as socializing, friendships, romantic relationships, advancing your career, speaking or otherwise performing in front of others, asserting yourself, using public bathrooms, being sexual, or even just being around others in a public place.

A momentary experience of social anxiety is completely normal, and in small measure, it's helpful. It keeps us sensitive to the feelings and concerns of others and thereby allows relationships and society to function. (Only very arrogant or psychopathic people rarely experience momentary social anxiety, because the feelings of others have little value to them.) But the lives of people with SAD are debilitated by their repeated experiences of social anxiety, resulting in lessened social and recreational satisfaction; fewer friendships and romantic relationships; lessened likelihood of being married; less success in school and career; and/or greater likelihood of experiencing depression.

Briefly list the ways your life has been held back by repeated experiences of social anxiety:

_____

_____

_____

_____

You are not alone! Social anxiety disorder is the third most common mental health problem in the United States. Research shows that 12% of adults have experienced SAD during their lives; 7% have experienced it in the past year. The prevalence is even higher among adolescents, 9% of whom have suffered from SAD in the past year (NIMH 2024). Sadly, only 37% of people with social anxiety disorder recover naturally (without treatment) during their lifetimes (Bruce et al. 2005). But the good news is that cognitive behavioral therapy (CBT) helps the large majority of people overcome SAD (Mayo-Wilson et al. 2014; de Ponti et al. 2024).

More Than a Phobia: The Role of Shame in Social Anxiety

Social anxiety disorder is also known as social phobia. A phobia is an exaggerated fear of a type of situation, animal, or object that is so anxiety provoking that it makes it very difficult to pursue important life activities or goals. This is true of social anxiety, too. Yet unlike all other phobias, social anxiety disorder typically stems from distorted, negative, shame-based core beliefs about yourself and how you believe you are perceived by others: that you are deficient in some fundamental way(s) and are not good enough to be liked, respected, loved, or successful. Other phobias stem from distorted, negative beliefs you have about the feared situation, animal, or object, such as dogs, rodents, elevators, heights, flying, and driving on freeways or bridges.

In this way, social anxiety disorder is fundamentally different from all other phobias: negative core beliefs about yourself and the shame they induce are driving, causal factors of social anxiety disorder for the vast majority of those who suffer from it. This is not true of other phobias. Through its evidence-based approach, this book will help you overcome social anxiety problems, replace shame with pride and self-confidence, and change your underlying core beliefs that are at the root of both social anxiety and shame.

What about Shyness and Introversion?

Is being shy different than being socially anxious? Well, not really. "Shyness" is a nonclinical word defined as: nervous or timid in the company of other people; slow or reluctant to do something (Oxford English Dictionary, s.v. "shyness") or easily frightened; disposed to avoid a person or thing (Merriam-Webster, s.v. "shyness"). So shyness is just another word for social anxiety. But being shy does not necessarily mean having social anxiety *disorder*, where the shyness makes it extremely difficult to pursue important activities or goals.

Social anxiety and shyness, however, are indeed different from introversion, although many people falsely conflate them. Introversion is a normal personality dimension in which a person generally desires less social stimulation and interaction than does a more extroverted person. Both introverts and extroverts may be socially anxious.

Measuring Your Social Anxiety and Shame

The National Social Anxiety Center (NSAC) has well-researched, self-scoring scales on its website, one measuring social anxiety and the other measuring shame. Find the links to these tools in the free tools: Resources at http://www.newharbinger.com/54322. Complete these questionnaires and record your scores below. Then, after completing this self-therapy program, you can fill out the same questionnaires again and see the before-and-after results measuring your progress.

- Leibowitz Social Anxiety Scale:

    anxiety score _____ avoidance score _____ total score _____ date _____

- External and Internal Shame Scale:

    score _____ date _____

Identifying Your Self-Therapy Goals

Review the ways you wrote that your life has been held back by social anxiety and shame. Now think about ways you would like your life to be different in the near future.

List below specific objective and subjective goals you would like to achieve—or make good progress toward—through your work in this self-therapy program. Objective goals are external and mainly behavioral, such as socializing, making friends, dating, applying for jobs, asserting yourself, engaging in public speaking, and performing. Make sure you identify things that are within your power to bring about. Subjective goals are internal and mainly about thoughts and feelings, such as feeling less anxiety and shame, feeling increased pride and self-confidence, and increasing self-esteem. Please list at least three objective goals and at least one subjective goal:

_____

_____

_____

_____

_____

_____

_____

A Little Courage and a Lot of Perseverance

You have to face your fears to learn to overcome them. Avoidance temporarily lessens your anxiety, but it increases your fear the next time you face a similar situation because it falsely teaches you that the risk was too grave for you to handle. By facing your fears, you learn that they are highly exaggerated and that you can handle them with your head held high: with pride and self-confidence rather than shame.

This takes courage. Courage does not mean being fearless. To the contrary, courage means choosing to do something despite the fact that you feel fear. The good news is that cognitive behavioral therapy is not macho therapy. It requires a little bit of courage because you'll be facing your fears in small steps. But remember that you're in charge: if a step ever feels too big and too scary, you can take a smaller step instead. You'll still be moving forward and making progress that way.

Taking a few small steps here and there doesn't get you very far, however. This self-therapy requires a lot of perseverance: taking small steps on a regular, frequent basis, ideally a little bit every day.

A little bit of courage and a lot of perseverance will bring you a long way toward achieving your self-therapy goals. Let's begin!

CHAPTER 2

Identifying Your Own Vicious Cycles

In the last chapter, we discussed common examples of vicious cycles of core beliefs, hot thoughts, and safety-seeking behaviors, all resulting in social anxiety and shame and reinforcing unhealthy core beliefs. Let's now identify and analyze the vicious cycles you unintentionally get caught up in so that we can develop strategies to break these cycles and overcome your social anxiety and shame.

Breaking It Down: Thoughts, Feelings, and Behaviors

The basic principle in CBT is that situations do not directly cause your feelings. It's the way you *think* about the situation that creates your feelings. Two different people could feel quite differently about the same situation because their perceptions of that situation are very different. And the same person may feel differently about a similar situation at two points in their life because their perceptions have changed over time. How you **feel** in reaction to a situation—past, present, or future—is a product of how you **think** about that situation and is greatly impacted by the way you **behave** in reaction to that situation: before, during, or after.

Let's examine your own cycles of thoughts, feelings, and behaviors when you experience social anxiety and shame. On the following worksheet, list three typical examples of situations in your life that trigger your social anxiety. These can be situations you've experienced in the recent past, situations you expect to be in in the future, or situations you avoid because of anxiety.

For each situation, write the feelings that you experience. Feelings include both emotions and physical sensations. Note that all feelings are single words or hyphenated words (e.g., anxious, embarrassed, self-conscious, jittery, sweaty). If you are writing whole sentences (e.g., "I felt like an idiot"), that is actually a hot thought, and it belongs in the following section. For each feeling, indicate its intensity from 0 to 100% at the time you were experiencing it. For future situations or situations that you've been avoiding, indicate how you expect you *would* feel if you actually *did* choose to engage in that situation.

In the third section for each situation, write down the hot (upsetting) thoughts that were going through your mind at the time you were experiencing these feelings. Thoughts may be words (self-talk), images (pictures going through your mind), and feared predictions. For each hot thought, indicate how strongly you believed it at the time you were feeling that way, from 0 to 100%.

In the last section for each situation, indicate the safety-seeking behaviors you rely on to try to cope with your anxiety. Remember, a safety-seeking behavior is something you do or avoid doing in an effort to try to prevent your hot thoughts from coming true. These behaviors may end up helping you or hurting you. Either way, write them down. Please note: some safety-seeking behaviors are external, such as avoidance, averting eye contact, speaking briefly, asking lots of questions, and hiding your shaky hands. Other safety-seeking behaviors are internal and relate to what you are focusing on, such as paying attention to your anxious feelings and symptoms in an effort to control them, scripting in your mind what to say next, critiquing in your mind how you think you're appearing and performing, and trying to guess the other person's thoughts and feelings about you. Even rumination is a safety-seeking behavior because you're probably trying to figure out if and how you screwed up so that you can do better next time.

Please read the following example worksheet, then take the time to thoughtfully complete the blank worksheet (which is also available at http://www.newharbinger.com/54322).

Triggering Situation Worksheet
(Example)

SITUATION in which you feel distressed, or that you avoid because of distress (past, present, or future):

- going to a party where I know few people

FEELINGS (intensity 0–100%)—emotions and physical sensations triggered by this situation:

- nervous: 90%   embarrassed: 50%   jittery: 50%
- tense: 75%   self-conscious: 100%

HOT THOUGHTS (strength of belief 0–100%)—the distressing words, images, or predictions on your mind when you are feeling this way:

- I won't know what to say, or I might say something stupid: 75%.
- I'll appear tense and nervous: 80%.
- People will think I'm weird and won't like talking to me: 100%.
- I've got to find a way out of this: 75%.

SAFETY-SEEKING BEHAVIORS—what you do or avoid doing to try to prevent your hot thoughts from coming true (including how you focus your attention):

- stay off by sidelines, look at my phone, and avert eye contact
- don't initiate conversations
- if someone talks to me: say very little, try to script what to say next, ask a lot of questions to keep attention off of me
- focus on my anxious feelings and symptoms to try to hide them

Triggering Situation Worksheet

Situation #1

SITUATION in which you feel distressed, or that you avoid because of distress (past, present, or future):

_____
_____

FEELINGS (intensity 0–100%)—emotions and physical sensations triggered by this situation:

_____
_____
_____

HOT THOUGHTS (strength of belief 0–100%)—the distressing words, images, or predictions on your mind when you are feeling this way:

_____
_____
_____
_____

SAFETY-SEEKING BEHAVIORS—what you do or avoid doing to try to prevent your hot thoughts from coming true (including how you focus your attention):

_____
_____
_____
_____

Situation #2

SITUATION in which you feel distressed, or that you avoid because of distress (past, present, or future):

_____
_____

FEELINGS (intensity 0–100%)—emotions and physical sensations triggered by this situation:

_____
_____
_____

HOT THOUGHTS (strength of belief 0–100%)—the distressing words, images, or predictions on your mind when you are feeling this way:

_____
_____
_____

SAFETY-SEEKING BEHAVIORS—what you do or avoid doing to try to prevent your hot thoughts from coming true (including how you focus your attention):

_____
_____
_____

Situation #3

SITUATION in which you feel distressed, or that you avoid because of distress (past, present, or future):

_____
_____

FEELINGS (intensity 0–100%)—emotions and physical sensations triggered by this situation:

_____
_____
_____

HOT THOUGHTS (strength of belief 0–100%)—the distressing words, images, or predictions on your mind when you are feeling this way:

_____
_____
_____

SAFETY-SEEKING BEHAVIORS—what you do or avoid doing to try to prevent your hot thoughts from coming true (including how you focus your attention):

_____
_____
_____

Core Beliefs: Your Bad Attitudes

Thinking happens at different levels. At the surface are **automatic thoughts** that pop into your mind in reaction to different situations that you're experiencing or reflecting on. If these automatic thoughts trigger anxiety, shame, depression, anger, or other upsetting feelings, they are called **hot thoughts**. Underlying your hot thoughts, and giving rise to them, are your ongoing attitudes—about yourself, about other people, and about the world—which are called **core beliefs**. Core beliefs act like eyeglasses that we wear: we are not usually paying attention to them, but they nevertheless greatly affect the way the world appears and feels to us. If we change our glasses (our core beliefs), the world feels and appears very different to us, even though the world itself hasn't changed at all. Unfortunately, it's harder to change core beliefs than glasses, but we will work on doing so throughout this book.

These core beliefs come in different forms and levels. At their deepest are **absolute beliefs** you have about yourself, about people in general, and about the way the world is or should be. Here are some examples:

I'm socially inept and bad at meeting people.

I'm fundamentally different and don't fit in.

Others see me as weird and uninteresting.

I should never offend or hurt anyone's feelings, even unintentionally.

Also very important are **conditional beliefs** (which are typically generated from your absolute beliefs): if-then ideas you have about yourself, other people and the world. Examples include:

If I make a social blunder, people will judge and reject me.

If my anxiety shows, people will think I am weak or weird.

If I displease or disagree with people, they'll dislike me.

If people knew what I was really like, they would dislike me.

Reread all the hot thoughts you wrote for the three situations in the previous exercise. Then, in the following spaces, write down *your core beliefs—about yourself, about other people, and about the world*—that give rise to your hot thoughts. Include both absolute beliefs and conditional beliefs. When doing so, please keep in mind that these beliefs are not the truth, but are the distorted, bad attitudes that have caused you so much anxiety and shame, and which we will actively work on changing throughout this self-therapy program.

_____

_____

_____

_____

_____

_____

_____

_____

Safety-Seeking Behaviors: Enemies in the Guise of Friends

Safety-seeking behaviors may seem like your friends: they purport to help you by reducing the risk that things go badly, and they may temporarily lessen your anxiety because you are reducing the risks. But safety-seeking behaviors are *false friends*—indeed, they are your enemies in the guise of friends—because they end up hurting you far more deeply and for far longer than the shallow and brief benefit you may experience from them. Relying on safety-seeking behaviors to cope with social anxiety is like an able-bodied person leaning on a crutch too much: while crutches may benefit you during a period of healing from an injury, leaning on them too long ends up making you weaker and dependent on them for longer. Worse yet, you end up believing that you are socially disabled and must always rely on crutches.

Let's first examine how this false-friend dynamic plays out with the most blunt of all safety-seeking behaviors: avoidance. When you avoid doing something because you experience anticipatory anxiety and hot thoughts about coming across badly and others reacting badly to you, you likely feel temporary relief from your anxiety since you know you won't be taking this risk. This is called negative reinforcement: avoidance reduces your anxiety, making it more likely you'll rely on avoidance to cope with anxiety in the future. But this benefit of anxiety reduction is short-lived. The anxiety is often replaced by shame when you believe yourself incapable of handling the situation. This shame may be accompanied by feelings of hopelessness and depression, thinking that you have further evidence that things won't get better in your life. In addition, avoidance may reduce your anxiety in the immediate present, but it actually *increases* your anxiety in the longer run because you reinforced your belief in your hot thoughts that led to the avoidance in the first place. You end up thinking that, were it not for avoidance, your fears would have come true.

You don't garner evidence that would help you learn that your hot thoughts are distorted: that in fact you can handle these situations well, and that most people will react positively, or at least neutrally, to you.

This same dynamic is true for the other safety-seeking behaviors you rely on. You may try to hide your anxiety symptoms from others. Or you may say and do things to keep others' attention off yourself. Maybe you engage in safety-seeking behaviors in your mind during an interaction: monitoring your anxiety symptoms, scripting what to say next, critiquing what you've said last, comparing yourself negatively to others, or desperately trying to mind-read the other person's thoughts and feelings toward you. You may also ruminate before or after social interactions: trying to figure out where you might have gone wrong in the hopes of creating a better impression the next time. Regardless of which safety-seeking behaviors you rely on, you end up reinforcing your belief in your hot thoughts. You're left feeling shame and lower self-confidence—despite whatever brief relief from anxiety your safety-seeking behaviors may have afforded you—which leads you to experience more anxiety and reliance on safety-seeking behaviors the next time.

And that's not all! Relying on safety-seeking behaviors tends to backfire: despite their purpose of trying to improve how you come across to others, the safety behaviors actually tend to *hurt* how you appear and converse, leading others to think you are uninterested or uninteresting.

So, as you can see, leaning on behavioral crutches is a major factor fueling your vicious cycle of social anxiety and shame. Throughout this self-therapy program, I'll guide you in identifying and gradually eliminating—or at least greatly reducing—your reliance on these false safety-seeking behaviors (Riccardi, Korte, and Schmidt 2017). This strategy will help you test your hot thoughts and core beliefs, gradually overcome social anxiety and shame, and build self-confidence and pride.

Review the safety-seeking behaviors you identified in the three situations you wrote in the Triggering Situation Worksheet. Perhaps you now realize that there are additional behavioral crutches you lean on in these situations, in which case add these to that worksheet. What is the impact of these safety-seeking behaviors—on how you come across, converse, perform, or feel—in both the immediate present and in the longer run?

_____

_____

_____

_____

_____

Doing Self-Therapy Homework Regularly

Starting now, each chapter in this book will close with suggestions for self-therapy homework for you to pursue during the coming week or two. You may be very eager to make as much progress as you can in as short a time as possible in order to relieve your suffering and move your life forward quickly. This is quite understandable given how much your life has been impacted by social anxiety and shame over the years! But in my experience, *CBT is vastly more effective for those who regularly practice the cognitive and behavioral skills and strategies than it is for those who simply read about these skills and strategies.* After all, you've been practicing the self-defeating core beliefs, hot thoughts, and safety-seeking behaviors for many years—for most of your life!—so they are deeply embedded in the neural pathways (wiring) in your brain. It will take a lot of practice to create and strengthen new neural pathways embodying healthier ways of thinking and behaving. You can rewire your brain in ways that will greatly diminish your social anxiety and shame and move your life forward, but to do so, you'll need to practice often.

I strongly recommend that, starting now, you **read only one chapter of this book each week, and spend the remainder of the week working on the self-therapy homework** presented at the end of each chapter. Following this strategy, I am confident that you will make much more progress toward your self-therapy goals. At this pace, it will take you about four months to complete the self-therapy process presented in this book: not a short time, certainly, but very quick compared to the many years you have struggled with social anxiety and shame during your life. It's well worth the investment of time and effort!

Self-Therapy Homework for the Coming Week

Visit http://www.newharbinger.com/54322 to download this worksheet.

Please complete the following worksheet, My Vicious Cycle, at least three times over the next week for situations that trigger your social anxiety or shame. These may be situations that occur during the week, or they may be past or future situations that are on your mind this week. First review the following completed example of this worksheet, then complete your own blank worksheet three times this week. (Blank worksheets are also available for download in the free tools.)

My Vicious Cycle Worksheet
(Example)

SITUATION (past, present, or future) that triggered/triggers your social anxiety or shame:

- making conversation with a stranger in a public place (e.g., a store, coffee shop, or standing in line)

FEELINGS (intensity 0–100%)—emotions and physical sensations triggered by this situation:

- nervous: 100%   self-conscious: 100%   hot: 75%
- tense: 100%   heart racing: 75%   sweaty: 40%

HOT THOUGHTS (belief 0–100%)—the distressing words, images, or predictions on your mind when you are feeling this way:

- They'll think I'm rude and am bothering them by speaking to them in a nonsocial situation: 100%.
- They'll notice me looking and sounding nervous and will think I'm weird: 100%.
- I won't know what to say, or will say something stupid: 100%.

CORE BELIEFS (absolute or conditional) about yourself, other people, or the world that are triggered in this situation:

- I'm socially unskilled, and I'm bad at meeting people and making small talk.
- It's weak and weird to be nervous interacting with people.
- I'm different and don't fit in.
- If someone I talk to seems uninterested, it means I made a bad impression on them.

SAFETY-SEEKING BEHAVIORS—what you do or avoid doing to try to prevent your hot thoughts from coming true (including how you focus your attention):

- Avoid initiating conversation with others.
- Avoid eye contact so they don't talk to me.

- If they initiate with me, I'll speak very briefly and then look away very quickly.
- Focus my attention on trying to control and hide my anxious symptoms and on scripting what to say right before I say it.

IMPACT of your safety-seeking behaviors on how you come across, converse, perform, or feel, in the immediate present and in the longer run:

- Looking away and avoiding initiating probably make me seem unfriendly or uninterested.
- Speaking briefly probably makes me seem uninterested and uninteresting.
- Scripting helps me have things to say, but probably comes across as awkward.
- Focusing on my anxiety ends up making me feel more anxious and distracts me from the conversation, making it harder to have things to say.

MY VICIOUS CYCLE WORKSHEET

SITUATION (past, present, or future) that triggered/triggers your social anxiety or shame:

_____

_____

FEELINGS (intensity 0–100%)—emotions and physical sensations triggered by this situation:

_____

_____

_____

HOT THOUGHTS (belief 0–100%)—the distressing words, images, or predictions on your mind when you are feeling this way:

_____

_____

_____

_____

CORE BELIEFS (absolute or conditional) about yourself, other people, or the world that are triggered in this situation:

_____

_____

_____

_____

SAFETY-SEEKING BEHAVIORS—what you do or avoid doing to try to prevent your hot thoughts from coming true (including how you focus your attention):

_____

_____

_____

_____

IMPACT of your safety-seeking behaviors on how you come across, converse, perform, or feel, in the immediate present and in the longer run:

_____

_____

_____

_____

CHAPTER 3

External Mindfulness: Getting Out of Your Head and into the Moment

So far, we've been discussing the vicious cycles that you unintentionally engage in that fuel your social anxiety and shame. Now we begin the process of learning and practicing a series of skills and strategies to break those vicious cycles so that you experience increased self-confidence and pride and achieve your self-therapy goals.

But first, let's review how your self-therapy homework went during the past week:

Were you able to identify the feelings, hot thoughts, core beliefs, and safety-seeking behaviors that you experience in situations that trigger your social anxiety or shame? Were you able to determine how your safety-seeking behaviors backfire and hurt you much more than whatever short-term benefit they may afford you? What did you learn in doing this exercise?

_____

_____

_____

If you did not do this exercise, or had trouble understanding or carrying it out, I suggest that you take your time, go back and review parts of the last chapter, and then try the exercise again. It's important to understand what constitutes your vicious cycles of social anxiety and shame so that you can develop effective strategies to break those cycles and help you achieve your self-therapy goals.

The first of these strategies is **external mindfulness**: learning to focus externally—on the person, conversation, and activity—with an attitude of curiosity, rather than focus internally on your thoughts, feelings, and behaviors with an attitude of self-judgment.

The Self-Conscious Actor

I'd like to illustrate the importance of external mindfulness by presenting an example of an actor with stage fright. Also called performance anxiety, stage fright is a type of social anxiety because it's centered on the fear of negative judgment.

Imagine a relatively new actor who, on opening night of her first professional performance in which she is playing the leading role, is experiencing a flood of social anxiety about how well she'll do and how well she'll be received. Not only is she the center of attention of a large audience full of strangers, but many of her friends and family members are also there, eager to watch her big night. In addition, there are a few professional theater critics in the audience who will write up their reviews of the play and her performance for the wider public to see.

Now imagine that this actor relies heavily on the safety-seeking behavior of self-focused attention in an effort to improve her performance as well as decrease her anxiety. While she is on stage performing her role, she focuses much of her attention on a stream of running commentary in her mind in which she is critiquing how she said certain lines or acted out certain elements of her performance. She sometimes also reminds herself of the next lines to say to avoid the humiliation she imagines in forgetting her lines or saying the wrong thing. At the same time, she carefully monitors the audience reaction: zeroing in on the coughing, the lack of laughter when she expected some, and other reactions that differ from what she had hoped for. She also focuses on her anxiety sensations—her sweaty brow and jittery hands—in an effort to control them, thinking that the audience notices her anxiety and judges her negatively for that.

In the space that follows, write what you believe the impact of this self-focused and self-critical attention is on this actor. How does it affect the way she feels and performs?

_____

_____

_____

What do you think is a more helpful way for the actor to focus her attention while performing and feeling anxious? How do you think that would help her?

_____

_____

_____

The Safety-Seeking Behavior of Self-Focused Attention

In addition to avoidance, self-focused attention is probably the most common safety-seeking behavior people rely on when they experience social anxiety. It's what is happening when you feel self-conscious: you are focusing on yourself in an effort to try to appear, converse, and perform better. But like other safety-seeking behaviors, self-focused attention backfires and ends up hurting the way you feel and come across more than the anxiety itself does!

Following is a list of the specific things you may be doing, and why, when you're engaging in the safety-seeking behavior of self-focused attention. Place a check beside those that are true for you:

- ☐ You focus on your anxious feelings and symptoms in an effort to try to control or hide them from others.

- ☐ You script in your mind what to say next in an effort to not run out of things to say, and to make sure that what you do say will be good enough.

- ☐ You self-censor things that pop into mind naturally in order to avoid the negative judgment you anticipate were you to say them.

- ☐ You critique in your mind what you just said or did in the hopes of doing better in the coming moments.

- ☐ You desperately try to read the reactions of the people around you in an effort to do better and avoid negative judgment.

Yet, as with all safety-seeking behaviors, whatever short-term benefits you may get from self-focused attention are greatly outweighed by the negative impact they have on how you feel, converse, and perform. Place a check beside the following negative impacts you often experience from self-focused attention when you're socially anxious:

- ☐ Focusing on your anxiety makes you feel more anxious, fueling a vicious cycle.

- ☐ Scripting what to say next distracts you from what is being said now, blocking things from popping into your mind spontaneously that you could say in reaction to what is being discussed. This makes it harder to keep your part of the conversation going.

- ☐ Scripting may also make you come across as awkward and stilted in conversation and harder for someone to connect with.

- ☐ While scripting or self-critiquing in your mind, you are probably looking away rather than looking at the speaker, giving them the impression that you're not interested.

- ☐ Self-censoring means you contribute less and reveal less, making it harder for someone to connect with you, and probably making you come across as less interested and interesting.

- ☐ Self-critiquing your appearance, conversation, or performance during an interaction only makes you feel more anxious and converse or perform less well. Little blips feel catastrophic. Self-critiquing distracts you and prevents you from participating more freely.

- ☐ When trying to read someone else's reaction, your negativity bias kicks in, which makes a neutral or even ambiguous response from someone seem terrible, leading you to feel more anxious and distracting you from participating more freely in the conversation or activity.

- ☐ Even when things go well during an interaction, you likely don't build self-confidence. Instead, having relied on self-focused attention leads you to think you dodged a bullet and will have to again lean on that crutch the next time in order to prevent disaster.

As you can see, *evaluating your performance and appearance while you are performing ends up hurting how you perform, converse, come across, and feel!*

The Helpful Alternative: External Mindfulness

Think about a conversation or other interaction you've had in which you felt minimal anxiety. Perhaps it involved someone you know with whom you're generally comfortable conversing or doing other activities. What was your attention focused on then?

_____

_____

In situations like these, how do you know what to say or do if you're not scripting it in your mind? How do you know how you're coming across if you aren't evaluating yourself during the conversation/activity?

_____

_____

_____

What you probably experience during an interaction in which you're not anxious is **external mindfulness**: the helpful alternative to the self-defeating safety-seeking behavior of self-focused and self-critical attention. *External mindfulness means getting out of your head and into the moment: focusing attention with curiosity on the person, conversation, and activity in the moment while treating any thoughts and feelings you have like background noise.* It may feel like a scary leap of faith to let go of the old crutch of self-focused attention that you're so used to leaning on when you're anxious. But by starting to practice external mindfulness in situations in which you experience only a little anxiety, and gradually practicing in harder and harder situations as you learn from experience how helpful this strategy is, it will become a new good habit for you that will lessen your anxiety and improve your conversation and performance.

The good news is, we all already have the skill of external mindfulness that we readily use when we're not anxious. For example, imagine you're somewhere you experience no anxiety, perhaps at a favorite restaurant with a good friend. Your attention is mainly focused externally, on what you are seeing and hearing in the moment. You will occasionally be distracted by things you hear and see around you: other people talking, other noise in the establishment, a police siren or car horn in the distance. But you're generally pretty good at noticing the distraction and then returning your attention back to the conversation or activity you had been focusing on. You don't have the ability to eliminate the distractions, but by treating them like background noise you can usually resume your conversation or other activity with minimal difficulty. This is an example of external mindfulness: you're engrossed in an activity you value by focusing externally in the present moment on what you see or hear (and in some situations, taste, touch, or smell) while treating distracting thoughts and feelings like unimportant background noise.

This is harder to do when you're anxious, of course, so it will take practice. Part of the inborn anxiety response is that it focuses your attention on the source of potential danger. When a deer is calmly munching away at vegetation in the forest and it suddenly hears a loud sound, it not only freezes and stops eating, but it also changes its focus away from the food and onto the source of potential danger: where the loud sound is coming from. Focusing on the danger is an adaptive response meant to protect you, so you can determine whether to freeze, flee, or fight. But with social anxiety, you think *you yourself* are the source of potential danger (that you'll make a bad impression), so you focus your attention on yourself. Rather than protecting you from danger—like the deer's change in focus from the food to the loud sound—your self-focused attention only makes you feel more anxious and hurts how you appear, converse, or perform.

Nowadays, when hearing the word mindfulness, I suspect most people think about meditation. Meditation and mindfulness are not the same thing. Meditation is simply one way to practice mindfulness. But when meditating, you are practicing *internal* mindfulness: focusing on your breathing, a mantra, imagery, or other thoughts and feelings. Meditation practice is useful for many things, certainly. However, many studies have demonstrated that meditation alone does not help most people overcome social anxiety (Mayo-Wilson et al. 2014), and is less effective than CBT in helping socially anxious people (Liu et al. 2021). Yet a great many studies have demonstrated that *external* mindfulness—aka attention training—is a critical component of the most effective treatment for social anxiety, cognitive behavioral therapy (Canvin, Janecka, and Clark 2016).

Curiosity Training to Practice External Mindfulness

How you pay attention to the person, conversation, or activity in the present moment is also important. When you're externally mindful, you're *paying attention with an attitude of curiosity (taking interest in) rather than judgment (evaluating as good or bad)*. An attitude of curiosity does not mean asking a barrage of questions. That's just a safety-seeking behavior aimed at having something to say and keeping attention off of yourself, which tends to annoy the other person (unless they're narcissistic). An attitude of curiosity rather than judgment means *focusing your attention on taking interest in the person, conversation, and activity, rather than evaluating how you think you're coming across.*

I like to call the strategy of practicing external mindfulness "curiosity training." I'll suggest ways for you to practice this skill throughout this program and beyond. While external mindfulness is not the only skill you'll need to overcome your social anxiety and shame, it is a foundational skill upon which all the other strategies are built.

The good news is that you don't have to be perfectly mindful: 100% external mindfulness is a fluke, not a realistic goal. Our brains evolved to be distractible so we can notice potential dangers on the periphery. The goal of curiosity training is to become overwhelmingly externally mindful when you are socially anxious. What I mean is that you're able to focus with interest on the person, conversation, or activity at least 75% of the time when you're feeling anxious; that you're aware when you slip into internal focus on your thoughts and feelings and are able to quickly return to an external focus; and that you become adept at treating your thoughts and feelings like background noise.

Nor does external mindfulness mean you never have negative thoughts or feelings. We don't have the ability to directly shut off thoughts, and trying to do so tends to make them stronger and cause them to stick around longer! It means not *engaging* the thoughts and feelings—treating them like background noise—and instead getting engrossed in the person, conversation, or activity in the moment.

Exactly What to Focus On

Sometimes it may not be clear what to focus your attention on when being externally mindful. Let's look more closely at how to be externally mindful with different types of social anxiety triggers:

- **Conversation:** When someone else is speaking, focus with interest on the person and what they're saying, and perhaps any other activity you may be doing together. When you're the one speaking, simply focus on *expressing* what you're saying with interest, *not* evaluating your performance or appearance.

- **Performance:** If you're speaking to a group, performing on stage, dancing when others can observe you, playing sports, or doing another activity or task in front of others, get mentally engrossed in what you're saying or doing. Treat any concerns about evaluating your performance like background noise.

- **Being sexual:** So called "sexual performance anxiety" is a type of social anxiety because it too is based on the fear of judgment, rejection, and embarrassment. Besides diminishing the pleasure of the experience, sexual anxiety can lead to sexual dysfunction, such as orgasmic inhibition, erectile disorder, or premature ejaculation. This problem is fueled by thinking of sex as a performance to be evaluated, rather than a mutual activity to be enjoyed. To be externally mindful during sexual situations, get mentally absorbed in any of the pleasurable sensations you're experiencing in the moment—touch, sight, sound, taste, and/or smell—while treating your concerns about evaluation and performance as background noise.

- **Shy bladder (paruresis):** Many people experience anxiety and difficulty urinating in certain bathroom situations, such as when others are present in the bathroom, are waiting to use the bathroom, or could be aware of how long you're taking to use the bathroom. For some people, this is a minor annoyance, but for others, this problem can be quite debilitating, making it hard to be away from "safe" bathrooms for more than a few hours. This problem is fueled by the distorted thought that people are focusing their attention on you and judging you for difficulty urinating. This leads you to focus your attention on your difficulty urinating, which makes you feel tense, and that muscle tension results in difficulty urinating! To practice external mindfulness in these situations, take your time and get engrossed in some other activity while you're in the bathroom—use your smart phone, read, listen to music/podcast/audiobook, plan the rest of your day, and so on—rather than focusing self-consciously on trying to urinate or being concerned about what others are thinking. Don't evaluate your "success" based on how long it takes you to urinate, or you are pressuring yourself and making it harder to urinate. Instead, get absorbed in some other activity that will take your mind off yourself and help relax you.

You can find further information about public speaking anxiety, male sexual performance anxiety, and shy bladder, as well as videos to practice curiosity training, in the free tools: Resources at http://www.newharbinger.com/54322.

Self-Therapy Homework for the Coming Week

Visit http://www.newharbinger.com/54322 to download the worksheets
and other materials for this chapter.

Throughout the next week, enhance your curiosity with the following external mindfulness exercises. Each time you practice, log what you did, and the percent that you were externally focused, in the External

Mindfulness Practice Log (below, and also available in the free tools: Worksheets). Logging your practice will help you see your progress and areas of difficulty, as well as motivate you to keep practicing.

1. Curiosity training while *observing*: Every day for about ten minutes, watch any video of your choosing—perhaps one specifically designed for attention training. (Links to the videos are available in the free tools: Resources.) Also practice curiosity training when you're people watching: go to a location with a variety of sights, sounds, and people you are not interacting with to just hang out and observe for at least ten minutes. Your goal is to get absorbed in all that you see and hear, slowly alternating your attention from one sight, sound, or person to another while treating your thoughts and feelings as background noise. Gently return your attention to what you see and hear whenever you're distracted by thoughts or feelings.

2. Curiosity training while *participating*: Every day for at least five minutes, focus mindfully (with an attitude of curiosity as opposed to judgment) during conversations or other activities you're participating in. Get mentally engrossed in the conversation or activity. Treat your thoughts and feelings like background noise. Whenever you're distracted, gently return your attention to taking interest in the person, conversation, or activity. Here are some helpful tips:

    a. Ideally start with conversations or activities in which you're pretty comfortable. Proceed to conversations or activities you're more anxious in as you get better at this.

    b. Practice this gently, patiently, and persistently. Don't criticize yourself or strain to be perfect. Accept that this is a process that will take time. Remember, the goal is not perfection, but being about 75% focused externally and with curiosity while also getting good at quickly returning your attention to the person, conversation, or activity whenever you slip into your thoughts and feelings.

    c. If you have difficulty remembering to practice, *turn your social anxiety into a cue*: whenever you feel anxious during an interaction, treat that anxiety as a reminder to get out of your head and focus externally on the person, conversation, or activity with curiosity.

External Mindfulness Practice Log

Date:	OBSERVING What did you observe?	What percent were you externally focused on what you were observing?	PARTICIPATING What was the conversation or activity?	What percent were you externally focused on the conversation or activity?

CHAPTER 4

Behavioral Experiments: Testing Your Anxious Hot Thoughts and Shame-Based Core Beliefs

Earlier, we discussed the vicious cycles you experience when you're feeling social anxiety or shame. We then began to work on changing one key element of that vicious cycle: replacing self-focused, self-critical attention with external mindfulness while adopting an attitude of curiosity rather than self-judgment. In this chapter, I'll introduce another crucial strategy to challenge and change two other key elements in your vicious cycles: behavioral experiments to test and modify your hot thoughts and core beliefs that cause you so much social anxiety and shame.

But first, let's discuss your self-therapy homework from this past week:

How has curiosity training (having an external mindful focus while observing and while participating) been going for you so far? How often have you been practicing? Have you kept a log of your practice, and what does it reveal about the progress you've been making and areas of difficulty you have?

_____

_____

_____

_____

This is a challenging skill to adopt, going against a lifelong habit of internal, self-critical attention when you're anxious. We'll continue practicing this crucial strategy every week through the remainder of this program. Be patient with yourself and persevere: it takes most socially anxious people several weeks before external mindfulness becomes a new habit. It'll get easier over time as you see that it lessens your anxiety and improves your conversation and performance.

Using the Scientific Method in Self-Therapy

People have a tendency to believe their disturbing thoughts. As you've seen, this is especially problematic for people experiencing social anxiety and shame—as well as depression, chronic anger, and other emotional problems—because thoughts are often distorted and contribute to making you feel worse and behaving in self-defeating ways. Cognitive behavioral therapy (CBT) teaches you to apply the scientific method to your disturbing thoughts: treat them as hypotheses that need to be tested through conducting experiments and gathering evidence. This process will help you modify your anxious hot thoughts and shame-based core beliefs, and you'll increase your self-confidence and pride as a result!

Do you focus on and often ruminate about your disturbing thoughts and the feelings they generate? If so, you probably assume these thoughts are likely true and so you behave accordingly; better safe than sorry! But, as we've discussed, this pattern simply fuels a vicious cycle, resulting in increased social anxiety and shame.

Instead, you can use the scientific method to *test* your anxious thoughts and shame-based core beliefs. Here are the steps:

1. Identify a specific activity you would like to engage in as an experiment to help you make progress toward one or more of your self-therapy goals. Choose an activity that triggers your social anxiety, but which you believe is not too hard for you to handle now. You can work on more challenging experiments later as you make further progress.

2. Identify your hot thoughts and core beliefs that get triggered when considering engaging in that activity, including the specific predictions you fear as a result.

3. Identify the safety-seeking behaviors you're tempted to rely on in an effort to prevent your feared predictions from coming true.

4. Identify constructive alternatives to your safety-seeking behaviors that you plan to utilize in your experiment in order to test your feared predictions, hot thoughts, and core beliefs.

5. Conduct one or more experiments in which you drop your safety-seeking behaviors and instead utilize the constructive alternative behaviors you identified.

6. Write down the evidence you gathered from your experiments, and analyze what you can learn as a result about your feared predictions, hot thoughts, and core beliefs.

7. Repeat these steps to continue making progress toward achieving your self-therapy goals.

Examples of Behavioral Experiments

How do you decide what experiments to conduct? The key is choosing activities to do as experiments that will help you make progress toward your self-therapy goals and also trigger your social anxiety. But remember to choose experiments that are no more challenging than you are willing to face now. You'll be able to choose more challenging ones later as you build more self-confidence through conducting experiments.

Let's take a look at common examples of activities used in behavioral experiments for social anxiety. These are just a sample; there are many other possibilities that you may prefer to work on to help you achieve your self-therapy goals.

- **Meeting people and socializing**: chat with coworkers; attend a group activity with new people (e.g., groups on meetup.com, classes and workshops, social groups, sporting groups, recreational groups, exercise groups, volunteering groups, hobby groups, religious groups, political and activist groups, professional or networking groups); greet and initiate conversations with people there; join small group conversations in progress; extend conversations longer; share contact information; initiate conversations with individuals in stores or other public locations; talk about common interests with strangers you meet on apps, listservs, and websites.

- **Making friends or dating:** initiate a phone or video conversation with someone you would like to get to know better; invite and go out with someone one on one; invite a small group of people to do something together; flirt or otherwise express interest in someone you're attracted to; converse with people on dating or social apps, then invite them out and meet in person; reveal more about yourself to someone you're wanting to get closer to; initiate physical intimacy with someone you're interested in.

- **Public speaking and other performing:** speak up in meetings at work or in community groups; take on a speaking role at church or in other community groups; give presentations at work or Toastmasters (https://www.toastmasters.org); volunteer to lead a meeting or discussion; be interviewed for jobs; dance at a club, party, or class; play a team sport; sing in a choir or at karaoke; call in on a radio talk show; post a video of yourself on social media singing, dancing, telling a story, or playing an instrument.

- **Possibly being observed by others:** take your time using public restrooms with others present or waiting to get in; place an order at a counter with others waiting; write or eat in front of others; eat alone in a restaurant without reading; make phone calls when others are in earshot; walk around crowded stores and neighborhoods; travel on crowded buses and trains.

- **Assertion:** tell a friend or date what restaurant or movie you would like to go to or what other activity you would like to do; express a contrary opinion to an individual or in a group discussion;

tell a server or counter service worker at a restaurant that you don't like something and would like to have it improved or replaced; return an item to a store; express your opinion or make a request to your boss.

Getting the Most out of Your Experiments

All experiments in CBT are structured as learning experiences. That is why we use the word "experiment," rather than another common term, "exposure." While you certainly are exposing yourself to anxiety-triggering situations during your experiments, you're doing so not simply to reduce your anxiety in the moment, but above all to test your hot thoughts and core beliefs that generate your anxiety and shame in the first place.

Over time, as your new learning is strengthened through conducting experiments, your anxiety and shame will gradually be replaced with increasing self-confidence and pride. In the very short run, however, it is likely that you will temporarily experience increased anxiety during your experiments as you begin to drop the crutches you're used to leaning on: your safety-seeking behaviors. But as you gain more and more evidence against your hot thoughts, feared predictions, and core beliefs—as you see people responding to you at least neutrally and often quite positively—your anxiety will quickly begin to diminish.

As you might expect, this week's self-therapy homework will include conducting your own behavioral experiment. The Experiment Worksheet included at the end of the chapter can help you get the most out of your experiments. The first portion of the worksheet, which helps you set up the experiment as a helpful learning experience, is completed before the experiment. The second portion of the worksheet—where you examine the evidence that was generated and then analyze what you can learn as a result to help you going forward—is completed after your experiment.

It may be tempting to skip doing the worksheet in order to save a little time and effort and simply conduct your experiment without any preparation or analysis. But doing so is likely to result in a less useful learning experience, as you may simply be repeating the old safety-seeking behaviors that you have relied on in the past. It is a worthy investment to spend the five to ten minutes needed to complete the first part of the worksheet before the experiment, and another five to ten minutes afterward using the worksheet to analyze what you can learn. Using this worksheet regularly for experiments you will conduct each week throughout this program will help you make more progress more quickly toward your self-therapy goals.

Take the time now to closely examine the example Experiment Worksheet that follows. Think through how you could use this worksheet to help you prepare for and then learn from an experiment you would want to do in the coming week.

Experiment Worksheet
(Example)

Before the Experiment

SELF-THERAPY GOAL(S) you are working on in this experiment:

- socializing more comfortably
- making new friends

EXPERIMENT you choose to do to make progress toward this goal:
(Choose something that triggers your social anxiety, but not so much that it feels too hard to face now.)

- attend a hiking group meetup

HOT THOUGHTS AND FEARED PREDICTIONS—what exactly you fear may happen when you conduct your experiment:
(Include specific, observable predictions.)

- I won't know what to say, or I might say something stupid.
- I'll appear tense and nervous.
- People will think poorly of me and won't enjoy talking to me.
- People will snicker at me, give me disapproving looks, and get out of the conversation quickly.

CORE BELIEFS (absolute or conditional) about yourself, other people, or the world that are triggered in this experiment:

- I'm bad at meeting people and socializing.
- If people see me blunder socially or appear nervous, they'll think I'm weird and uninteresting and will reject me.

SAFETY-SEEKING BEHAVIORS—what you do or avoid doing to try to prevent your hot thoughts from coming true (including how you focus your attention):

- Avoid going.
- Stand off on the edges so I minimize interacting with people.

- Just say hi to people and look away so I don't have to talk to them.
- If someone does talk to me: keep my responses very brief, and script in my mind questions to ask so that I keep the attention off of me and have something to say.
- Self-monitor my anxiety symptoms in an effort to control or hide them.
- Criticize myself harshly in my mind after every perceived blunder.

BEHAVIORAL GOALS FOR THIS EXPERIMENT—specific action steps you plan to take during the experiment to test out your hot thoughts, feared predictions, and core beliefs:

(Include external mindful focus and other helpful alternatives to all your safety-seeking behaviors.)

- Attend, and arrive about ten minutes early so I can start interacting when fewer people are there.
- Stand in the midst of people; smile and say hello to people, and don't look away for a couple seconds.
- Initiate conversations with three people.
- During conversations, focus mindfully on what is being said with curiosity while treating my thoughts and feelings like background noise.
- Say a few sentences at a time instead of just a few words.
- Pat myself on my back after every interaction, no matter how imperfect.

After the Experiment:

EVIDENCE: What exactly happened during your experiment? Did your hot thoughts and feared predictions come true? If so, how bad was it and how did you cope with it?

- Two people initiated conversation with me.
- I initiated three conversations and joined one group conversation already in progress. I stayed in the conversations anywhere from three to twenty minutes.
- At a few points, I stumbled on my words, or there were awkward pauses because I didn't know what to say. But then the conversation just continued, and no one gave me a negative look or abruptly ended the conversation.

- Although I felt very nervous at first, I started relaxing and even enjoying a couple of the conversations as we clicked on things we had in common.

WHAT YOU LEARNED: What did this experiment tell you about yourself, your hot thoughts, and your core beliefs? How can you build on this going forward?

- If I approach people, focus mindfully, and speak longer, I'm pretty good at making social conversation, and some people enjoy talking to me.
- A little awkwardness or a few blunders with a new person is no big deal.

Bonus Supplements

In the free tools: Bonus Chapter Supplements at http://www.newharbinger.com/54322, you'll find two optional sections for this chapter you may find helpful, which are described below:

Building Confidence in Your Social Skills

You may be questioning whether you're ready to do experiments because you believe your social skills aren't good enough. It's a very common core belief among socially anxious people that they are socially inept generally, or at least poor at specific social skills, such as meeting people, making small talk, and developing friendships. In fact, you may believe your social anxiety is actually *caused* by being deficient in social skills. Yet, in reality, the large majority of socially anxious people exercise normal social skills when they are not very anxious. The problem is that relying on self-focused attention and other safety-seeking behaviors when you're anxious prevents you from fully using the social skills you already have, and often hurts how you come across. You can conduct experiments in which you drop your safety-seeking behaviors to test out your core belief that you're socially unskilled and to see how well you connect with others.

Even if you haven't strongly developed certain social skills due to a long history of relying on the safety-seeking behavior of avoidance, you probably actually have good ideas as to what to do in those challenging situations. Or perhaps you're neurodivergent and experience interactions differently than neurotypical people do. Either way, practicing these skills will increase your self-confidence and decrease your anxiety.

To learn how to use experiments to build confidence in your social skills, read Bonus Supplement #1 for this chapter: http://www.newharbinger.com/54322.

Conducting Surveys as Experiments

You may be tempted to dismiss the positive evidence you garner during your experiments by telling yourself that the other people were just being nice, that they may be *thinking* badly of you and are just too polite to react badly toward you. To help you test out your fears of what others think, you may find it beneficial to conduct one or more informal surveys in which you ask several people what they think in reaction to a few questions that you design beforehand. To learn how to conduct surveys to test your fears, read Bonus Supplement #2 for this chapter: http://www.newharbinger.com/54322.

Self-Therapy Homework for the Coming Week

Visit http://www.newharbinger.com/54322 to download the worksheets and other materials for this chapter.

1. Choose and carry out at least one experiment to work on one or more of your self-therapy goals. Before and after each experiment, complete the Experiment Worksheet (below and in the free tools). It's sometimes helpful to repeat an experiment multiple times during the week, in which case just complete the worksheet once, and describe the evidence you garnered from each time you conducted the experiment. Don't drink alcohol or take cannabidiol (CBD), benzodiazepines, or beta blockers right before or during your experiments. Using any of these is a safety-seeking behavior that will limit your learning and progress.

2. Continue to practice curiosity training every day for at least five minutes, especially during interactions in which you're anxious, including your experiments. (See chapter 3 if you need a reminder.) Keep a record of your practice and your progress and difficulties with this skill. Use the External Mindfulness Practice Log in the free tools: Worksheets.

Experiment Worksheet

Before the Experiment:

SELF-THERAPY GOAL(S) you are working on in this experiment:

_____

_____

EXPERIMENT you choose to do to make progress toward this goal:

(Choose something that triggers your social anxiety, but not so much that it feels too hard to face now.)

_____

_____

HOT THOUGHTS AND FEARED PREDICTIONS—what exactly you fear may happen when you conduct your experiment:

(Include specific, observable predictions.)

_____

_____

_____

_____

_____

_____

_____

CORE BELIEFS (absolute or conditional) about yourself, other people, or the world that are triggered in this experiment:

_____

_____

_____

SAFETY-SEEKING BEHAVIORS—what you do or avoid doing to try to prevent your hot thoughts from coming true (including how you focus your attention):

_____

_____

_____

_____

_____

BEHAVIORAL GOALS FOR THIS EXPERIMENT—specific action steps you plan to take during the experiment to test out your hot thoughts, feared predictions, and core beliefs:

(Include external mindful focus and other helpful alternatives to all your safety-seeking behaviors.)

_____

_____

_____

_____

_____

After the Experiment:

EVIDENCE: What exactly happened during your experiment? Did your hot thoughts and feared predictions come true? If so, how bad was it and how did you cope with it?

_____

_____

_____

_____

_____

_____

WHAT YOU LEARNED: What did this experiment tell you about yourself, your hot thoughts, and your core beliefs? How can you build on this going forward?

_____

_____

_____

_____

_____

_____

CHAPTER 5

Being a Good Parent to Yourself: Counteracting Self-Critical Rumination

So far in this program, we've looked at your vicious cycle of social anxiety and shame, and we've begun working on two crucial strategies aimed at breaking key elements of your vicious cycle: (1) having an external mindful focus with an attitude of curiosity to counteract self-focused, self-critical attention; and (2) conducting behavioral experiments to test and change anxious hot thoughts and shame-based core beliefs. In this chapter, I present a strategy to counteract self-critical rumination—beating yourself up for imperfection and worrying about what someone else may think of you—which fuels your vicious cycles and deepens your social anxiety and shame.

Let's first review how your self-therapy homework has been going:

Did you do one or more experiments and complete the Experiment Worksheet before and after them? What evidence did you garner countering your hot thoughts and core beliefs? What did you learn?

_____
_____
_____
_____
_____

How are you doing in developing the skill of focusing your attention externally, with curiosity, on the person, conversation, or other activity, while treating your thoughts and feelings like background noise?

Are you making progress utilizing your anxious feelings as a reminder to get out of your head and return your attention to the external moment?

_____

_____

_____

Please don't worry or feel dismayed if you're having difficulty conducting experiments or being externally mindful when you're anxious. It's part of a process, and you'll continue practicing these strategies every week throughout the remainder of this program…and hopefully throughout your life! But if you haven't been practicing, you'll make much more progress if you go back and spend a week working on the self-therapy homework from the last chapter before proceeding with the new strategy described in this chapter. Be patient and persevere. There's no hurry. This program is about changing unhelpful, long-term patterns, and that takes time and practice.

Rumination: The Fuel for Social Anxiety and Shame

Place a check by any of the following thinking patterns you experience:

- ☐ Before an interaction you feel anxious about, you worry a lot about how you'll do and the impression you'll make.

- ☐ After a challenging interaction, you brood and beat yourself up a lot about things you said or did that you think may have created a bad impression.

- ☐ After a challenging interaction, you worry a lot about what the other person(s) might be thinking of you based on how you performed or appeared.

- ☐ Before, during, or after challenging interactions, you compare yourself negatively to others who you think perform or appear better than you, or whom you believe others like or respect more than you.

All these are forms of **rumination**: repeatedly mulling over upsetting thoughts before, during, or after anxiety-provoking interactions. Rumination fuels your social anxiety and shame: it makes you feel miserable while you're doing it, and it sets you up for feeling more anxious and self-conscious the next time you face similar interactions.

Whether you think of it as ruminating, worrying, brooding, beating yourself up, or comparing yourself to others, almost everyone with social anxiety disorder does this at times. Sometimes you may ruminate off and on for many years after an interaction, feeling even worse about it than when it first occurred!

Why Do You Ruminate?

If ruminating only makes you feel more anxiety and shame, why do you keep doing it? You may believe you simply cannot stop ruminating—that it's a bad habit that you have no control over. Well, ruminating certainly *is* a bad habit that probably began early in your life. But indeed, you can choose to do something else instead of ruminating. I'll illustrate this with the following thought experiment:

Imagine that you've been beating yourself up for an extended period about something you said or did during a recent interaction, and worrying that the other person is now thinking badly of you. You're feeling much anxiety and shame while embroiled in all this ruminating. And then your phone rings and you see that it's a good friend whom you've been playing phone tag with for quite some time, and whom you'd really love to talk to. Think about the following:

- What would you do when you see your friend is calling you?
- What would you be focusing your attention on while you do that?
- How would you be feeling while you do that?

Chances are, you'd stop ruminating and have a conversation with your friend. You'd probably focus your attention on the conversation you're having, and not on your previous upsetting thoughts. Although your anxiety and shame would likely linger a bit in the background, you'd probably soon feel much better during the phone conversation.

In other words, *you can stop ruminating if you choose, instead, to focus your attention mindfully on some other activity that you value, while treating your distressing thoughts and feelings like background noise.*

If rumination is an old bad habit, but one that you can choose to set aside to do something else that matters to you, the question arises: why do you still ruminate? Rumination is like a computer that is stuck trying to execute an operation but keeps spinning and spinning…and getting nowhere. The computer is trying to accomplish something, but it's stuck. That's what our brain is doing when we ruminate. (At least the computer isn't feeling anxiety and shame as a result!) Write your answers to these questions here:

What do you believe you are trying to accomplish when you ruminate?

_____

_____

_____

How well do you accomplish this desired goal when you ruminate?

_____

_____

What are the effects of ruminating on the way you feel and behave, in the present and in the future?

_____

_____

_____

You may hope that worrying or beating yourself up will help you come across better in the future. And you may hope that, by comparing yourself negatively to others whom you admire, you'll motivate yourself to make improvements.

Regardless of these hopes, you probably have come to realize that you actually get little or nothing positive out of ruminating. You only end up feeling worse about yourself, both in the moment, as well as the next time you face a similar experience. In sum, *ruminating is another safety-seeking behavior that backfires on you. It's intended to help you improve how you come across, but it only makes you feel more social anxiety and shame.*

The Bad Parent and Good Parent Analogy

Consider this analogy: a child comes home from elementary school one day and eagerly shows their parent a writing project they just completed. The parent looks at it and says: "Well, this is okay, but I know you can do so much better! I bet your friend Julie worked harder and did a better job than you did. I'm disappointed in you, and I'm sure your teacher is, too!"

Even if the parent is genuinely motivated by a desire to help the child improve, such treatment is likely to backfire. Maybe the child will work harder and harder for a while to please their parent, but if this is how they are repeatedly treated, they'll likely develop the core beliefs that they're fundamentally deficient and that they have to perform perfectly in order to be accepted. Their self-esteem and mood are likely to be damaged, and they'll probably experience a lot of social anxiety and shame going forward.

Contrast this with a different parent who tells the child: "I'm so proud of you! You did such a beautiful job! You worked hard on this, and it shows how much you've learned. You're becoming a better and better writer each time! And you know what? I can think of a way you can do even better in the future. Next time you could give an example to help get your point across even better." If this is the way the parent generally responds to the child's school efforts, that fortunate child is likely to develop the core beliefs that they're worthwhile, and they don't have to be perfect in order to be accepted. And, to top it off, they're likely to improve their performance going forward!

When you ruminate—whether by being self-critical, worrying about how others perceive you, or comparing yourself negatively to others—you're treating yourself like the bad parent in this analogy treats their child, and you suffer similar consequences: increased social anxiety and shame and worsened performance. You can, however, retrain your mind to be a good parent to yourself. Using this strategy regularly will decrease your social anxiety and shame and improve how you feel and do in the future.

Steps to Being a Good Parent to Yourself

Follow these steps every time you (a) do something anxiety provoking, such as a self-therapy homework experiment; (b) become self-critical or worried about how you come across; or (c) compare yourself negatively to others.

1. Write down all the positive things you did, no matter how small or imperfect. *Begin each entry with the words "I'm proud that..." Be specific and detailed, as that will help you believe what you write.*

   Example: "I'm proud that I attended. I'm proud that I stayed two hours, which is much longer than I usually do. I'm proud that I smiled at and greeted several people. I'm proud that I initiated a few conversations. I'm proud that I extended one conversation for more than ten minutes. I'm proud that I asserted a different opinion. I'm proud that I tried to focus mindfully on the conversation."

2. If there was anything you think you didn't do so well, do not criticize yourself for it. Instead, turn it into a constructive learning experience by writing down the specific behavioral steps you want to take next time. *Use the phrase "I want" rather than something self-critical, like "I should."* Importantly, don't jump to this step until you've affirmed the positive things you did by doing step 1 first.

   Example: "Next time, I want to speak more about myself and talk a little longer each time I speak up. I also want to share contact information with someone I've enjoyed talking to."

3. Then, as soon as possible, choose an activity that you value to engage in, and focus mindfully on that activity—get engrossed in it—while treating your unpleasant thoughts and feelings like background noise.

4. Whenever you're bothered again by self-criticism or worry about the same situation, remind yourself that you've already learned what you can from that experience, and that rumination only makes you feel miserable. Then refocus your attention on getting engrossed in an activity you value while treating your thoughts and feelings like background noise.

Don't wait until you start ruminating before following these steps. Instead, create a new habit of proactively following these steps after each challenging experience you have (e.g., a self-therapy homework experiment or any other life activity that triggered your social anxiety). And don't disqualify the positive things you did (e.g., "It wasn't good enough," "Anyone can do that," or "It's no big deal"). Each positive step deserves a pat on the back, and doing so will help you feel better and do better next time!

Let's practice the first two steps of being a good parent to yourself now. Pick a challenging experience that you've been ruminating about lately:

Challenging experience:

_____

Step 1: Finish the sentence "I'm proud that…" (List specific things you did then that were positive, no matter how small or imperfect.)

_____

_____

_____

_____

_____

Step 2: Finish the sentence "Next time I have a similar experience, I want to try to…" (List specific things that you want to continue doing, or do differently next time, based on what you learned in this experience last time.)

_____

_____

_____

Self-Therapy Homework for the Coming Week

Visit http://www.newharbinger.com/54322 to download the worksheets for this chapter.

1. Practice being a good parent to yourself every day for any situation that triggers anxiety, shame, rumination, or comparing yourself to others. Definitely practice this after doing your behavioral experiments this week. Use the Being a Good Parent to Yourself Worksheet (below and in the free tools).

2. Choose and carry out one or more experiments to work on one of your self-therapy goals. Use the Experiment Worksheet in the free tools before and after your experiments.

3. Continue to practice having an external, mindful focus. Whenever you feel anxious around others, interpret that anxiety as a reminder to focus your attention externally and with curiosity on the person, conversation, and activity while treating your thoughts and feelings like background noise.

Being A Good Parent To Yourself Worksheet

Complete this worksheet every time you (a) do something anxiety provoking, such as a self-therapy homework experiment; (b) become self-critical or worried about how you come across; or (c) compare yourself negatively to others.

1. Write down all the positive things you did, no matter how small or imperfect. Begin each entry with the words "I'm proud that…" Be specific and detailed, as that will help you believe them.

    Challenging situation: _____

    I'm proud that… _____

    _____

    _____

    _____

    _____

    _____

    _____

2. If there was anything you think you didn't do so well, don't criticize yourself for it. Instead, turn it into a constructive learning experience by writing down the specific behavioral steps you want to take next time. Use the phrase "I want" rather than something self-critical, like "I should." Importantly, don't jump to this step until you've affirmed the positive things you did by doing step 1 first.

    Next time, I want… _____

    _____

    _____

3. Then, as soon as possible, choose an activity that you value to engage in, and focus mindfully on that activity—get engrossed in it—while treating your unpleasant thoughts and feelings like background noise.

4. Whenever you're bothered again by self-criticism or worry about the same situation, remind yourself that you've already learned what you can from that experience, and that rumination only makes you feel miserable. Then refocus your attention on getting engrossed in an activity you value while treating your thoughts and feelings like background noise.

CHAPTER 6

Reframing: Making Your Thoughts Realistic, Helpful, and Compassionate

Because your social anxiety and shame stem from the way you think, much of this self-therapy program so far has been focused on identifying and modifying your self-defeating thinking patterns. In this chapter, I introduce you to an additional strategy called reframing to help you change your thinking so that it's realistic, constructive, and self-compassionate.

But first, let's discuss your experience with the self-therapy homework recently:

How has your practice of being a good parent to yourself been going and feeling for you? Has this helped you lessen your self-critical rumination and begin to take pride in the progress you're making, however imperfect? Please give some examples.

_____

_____

_____

_____

How have your recent experiments been going? What evidence have you gathered to counter your hot thoughts and underlying core beliefs? What are the key lessons you've learned from these experiments?

_____

_____

_____

_____

Are you continuing to practice and strengthen the skill of external mindful focus whenever you're anxious? How has that been going?

_____

_____

_____

Don't let perfectionism frustrate or demoralize you. These are challenging strategies in which you're changing old thinking and behavior patterns that you've had for most of your life. Be patient and perseverant. We'll continue practicing these strategies throughout this program, and over time they'll become healthy new habits for you.

Reframing Strategies

Reframing (aka cognitive restructuring) is aimed at modifying your thinking so that it is truer, more helpful, and self-compassionate (Hope, Heimberg, and Turk 2019). There are several different reframing strategies, and we've already been working with two of them. Using experiments to test the validity of your hot thoughts and underlying core beliefs, and to modify them accordingly, is a very powerful reframing strategy. So is being a good parent to yourself because you're learning to notice and affirm the positive steps you take, despite whatever imperfections. In this chapter, we'll discuss other reframing strategies that you may find helpful.

Many socially anxious people find that the two reframing strategies you've already learned are sufficient for their progress, and they don't feel the need for additional strategies to modify the thinking that makes them feel anxiety and shame. But there are specific situations and times when you may find that the additional reframing strategies presented in this chapter will help you make further progress in:

- reducing anticipatory anxiety, increasing motivation, and decreasing avoidance;
- overcoming rumination, including worry;
- overcoming upsets and depression; and
- accepting uncertainty (e.g., about how things will go or what others think of you).

Reframing is *not* the same as the "power of positive thinking." While positive thinking is often more helpful than negative thinking, not every experience in life is positive, of course. If you try to make yourself feel better by telling yourself something positive when you don't believe it, you're likely to cringe and not feel any better. It may even backfire and make you feel worse; this is because it might trigger further shame-based thinking like "That may be true for some people, but not for me" or "How pathetic I am that I have to tell myself things like this!"

The biggest challenge in doing reframing effectively is coming up with a constructive, believable attitude to counter your hot thoughts—one that is realistic, helpful, and self-compassionate. Following are four reframing strategies for you to try.

Strategy 1: The True-However-Therefore Reframing Formula

This reframing strategy uses the following formula:

- **It's true that...** (followed by a *brief* summary of the evidence that supports your hot thought, minus any distortions, exaggerations, or degrading comments)
- **However...** (followed by a more detailed summary of the evidence that refutes your hot thought)
- **Therefore...** (followed by a statement you find believable describing what would be a more helpful and self-compassionate way for you to view this situation)

For example, let's say you struggle with the anxious thought "I might mess the conversation up, act nervous and weird, and make a bad impression." Using the true-however-therefore formula, your constructive attitude might be: "*It's true that* sometimes I'm awkward and nervous in conversation, and that not everyone likes me. *However*, I'm usually able to converse pretty well when I choose to focus on what we're saying with curiosity. I've also noticed that, even when I do act awkwardly in a conversation, the other person doesn't seem to have a negative reaction and we just keep on talking. Besides, I occasionally notice other people say something silly and act awkwardly, and I don't care much at all. No one is liked by everyone, and I don't like everyone, either! *Therefore*, I'm going to focus with curiosity on the conversation and the person, and give it a chance. If the person doesn't seem to like me, that just means we have different tastes and we're not a good match. So I'll move on to talk to someone else."

Now, try this on your own by completing the following worksheet (also available in the free tools).

True...However...Therefore... Reframing Worksheet

Hot thought (when you feel anxious, shame, or depressed)

_____

_____

It's true that... (brief summary of the evidence that supports your hot thought, minus any distortions, exaggerations, or degrading comments)

_____

_____

_____

However... (a more detailed summary of the evidence that refutes your hot thought)

_____

_____

_____

_____

_____

Therefore... (a statement you find believable describing what would be a more helpful and self-compassionate way for you to view this situation)

_____

_____

➤ After completing this worksheet, refocus mindfully on activities you value while treating your thoughts and feelings like background noise.

Strategy 2: Acceptance and Problem Solving

This reframing strategy is helpful when you find yourself worrying about the possibility of something upsetting happening. It involves writing out a constructive attitude of *acceptance* (of that which you cannot control or change) and *problem solving* (of that which you may be able to change or influence). Make sure you do these steps in writing, as trying to do so in your head could foster further rumination.

1. Identify what aspects of the situation you're worrying about that are beyond your control, and what aspects you may be able to change or influence.

2. Write a statement of acceptance for those things you can't control or change. Acceptance doesn't mean you *like* something; it simply means you acknowledge it does (or may) exist and that you can live with it and move on.

3. For those things that you may be able to change or influence, engage in problem solving by writing out action steps you plan to pursue and when you plan to take these steps.

For example, let's say that you're anxious about the possibility of some people reacting negatively to you or treating you as a stereotype because of your perceived race, ethnicity, religion, sexual orientation, gender, age, disability, appearance, or any other quality that some people have prejudices about. Using the acceptance and problem-solving approach, your constructive attitude may be "I accept that I don't have any control over other people's thoughts and feelings, including whether they are prejudiced. If someone seems to dislike me for who I am, or treats me like a stereotype, I accept that this is a reflection of some problem this person has, and, although it's unpleasant, it says nothing about my worth, or my likability to nonprejudiced people. Depending on how safe and bold I feel in that situation, I can correct the person or assert that their comment is offensive; or I can simply walk away with my head held high, and move on to talk to someone else who hopefully will be more pleasant and less prejudiced."

Or, if you're worrying about how well you'll perform and appear in a job interview or a work presentation, you could apply the acceptance and problem-solving approach in this manner: "No matter how well I perform and how confident I appear, I accept that I cannot control their thoughts and feelings about me. So instead, I'll focus mindfully on what I and others are saying, ignore my anxious thoughts and feelings, and be proud of what I'm doing, no matter how imperfectly. I may also be able to learn something useful from this experience that will help me going forward."

Now, it's your turn to practice. Complete the following worksheet (also available in the free tools):

Acceptance and Problem Solving Reframing Worksheet

Situation that you have been worrying about

_____
_____

Most distressing hot thoughts (up to three) triggered by this situation

_____
_____
_____
_____
_____
_____
_____

ACCEPTANCE: I need to accept that... (aspects of this situation that are beyond your control or influence)

_____
_____
_____

PROBLEM SOLVING: aspects of this situation that you can change or influence, including your reactions, along with helpful action steps and when you'll do them

_____

_____

_____

_____

_____

_____

_____

➤ After completing this worksheet, refocus mindfully on these steps or other activities you value while treating your thoughts and feelings like background noise.

Strategy 3: The Three Cs

This reframing strategy uses three simple steps. It can be done in writing or through self-talk out loud. It's best not to try this approach silently in your thoughts, as that may foster rumination.

1. **CATCH IT:** Identify your hot thought(s) when you're experiencing anxiety, shame, another negative feeling, or avoidance.

2. **CHECK IT:** Identify all the evidence in that situation—what actually happened and other facts—that supports or refutes your hot thoughts.

3. **CHANGE IT:** Identify a constructive attitude: a realistic, helpful, and compassionate alternative to your hot thoughts. Identify action steps you'll take and when you'll do them. Then refocus mindfully on these steps or other activities you value while treating your thoughts and feelings like background noise.

Read this example of the Three Cs in action, and reflect on how you could use this strategy for your own concerns:

CATCH IT: I made a fool of myself by saying something stupid at a work meeting.

CHECK IT: Someone corrected what I said in a matter-of-fact manner, and then the discussion continued on as if nothing bad had happened. No one said or did anything to indicate a negative reaction to me. In fact, a coworker started making small talk with me right after the meeting.

CHANGE IT: No one expects me to be perfect, just like I don't expect that of others. I'll go out of my way to chat with coworkers daily, and I'll focus mindfully on the conversation and on my work.

Practice the Three Cs strategy here by completing the following worksheet (also available in the free tools) about one specific situation you've been feeling anxiety or shame about:

The Three Cs Reframing Worksheet

CATCH IT: Identify your hot thoughts when feeling bad or avoiding.

_____

_____

CHECK IT: Identify all the evidence supporting and refuting your hot thoughts.

_____

_____

_____

_____

_____

CHANGE IT: Identify a constructive attitude: a realistic, helpful, and compassionate alternative to your hot thoughts that you find believable. Identify action steps you'll take and when you'll do them.

_____

_____

_____

_____

_____

➤ After completing this worksheet, refocus mindfully on these steps or other activities you value while treating your thoughts and feelings like background noise.

Strategy 4: Very Brief Oral Reframing

If you have a repeated pattern of distorted hot thoughts, identify a short statement of a self-compassionate and constructive attitude that you believe at your best of times. For example, if you repeatedly criticize yourself harshly for perceived mistakes, you might use a statement such as "I don't have to be perfect; no one does" or "I accept myself as I am, imperfections and all." Or you might simply say, "Oh, well!" and shrug it off. If you repeatedly compare yourself negatively to others, you might use "Everyone has strengths and weaknesses." If you repeatedly worry about things, consider using "I'll do the best I can; no one can make everything turn out perfect."

A variant of this strategy is to simply label your thought in a way that makes it easier to treat it as background noise and refocus mindfully on something you value. For example: "That's just anxious (or depressive) noise" or "That's just an old tape/message" or "I refuse to let my thoughts hold me back in life." Or simply: "Blah, blah, blah."

Whenever you notice you're engaging in the targeted hot thoughts (e.g., self-criticism, negative self-comparison, or repetitious worry), recite your short constructive attitude statement. Do so out loud and with a confident tone if you're alone, as that's more effective. Then, refocus on an activity you value and treat your thoughts and feelings like background noise.

Until this brief reframing strategy becomes a new habit, try carrying the short constructive attitude statement with you (e.g., on your phone or a card in your wallet). You may also find it helpful at first to wear or carry a symbolic reminder of your constructive attitude (e.g., a special piece of jewelry, a rubber wrist band, a religious object, a pretty stone).

To get started, write your initial ideas of very brief constructive attitude statements you could say to yourself when you're disturbed by hot thoughts:

_____

_____

_____

_____

_____

Bonus Supplement: In-Depth Reframing

If you ever find that the above reframing strategies aren't sufficiently helpful—that your mood doesn't improve significantly or you continue to ruminate or avoid—then try the In-Depth Reframing Worksheet described in the free tools: Bonus Chapter Supplements at http://www.newharbinger.com/54322.

Warning about all Reframing Strategies

Don't criticize yourself for having hot thoughts, or paradoxically you'll end up strengthening them. Everyone has hot thoughts. You don't have control over whether or not your brain generates a hot thought. The goal of reframing is *not* to stop having hot thoughts. No one can accomplish this goal; nor is it necessary. *The goal of reframing is to disbelieve your hot thoughts so you can view them as passing mental noise and not take them seriously, and instead refocus mindfully on activities you value.* The less you pay attention to your hot thoughts, the less they bother you and the sooner they'll fade away into the background. The more you engage your hot thoughts, the stickier and more oppressive they become.

Self-Therapy Homework for the Coming Week

Visit http://www.newharbinger.com/54322 to download the worksheets and other materials for this chapter.

1. Practice using one or more of the reframing strategies introduced in this chapter whenever you feel strong anxiety or shame, are ruminating, or are avoiding. Download and complete the reframing worksheets in the free tools.

2. Choose and carry out one or more experiments to work on one of your self-therapy goals. Use the Experiment Worksheet in the free tools before and after your experiments.

3. Practice being a good parent to yourself after your experiments this week and for any situation that triggers anxiety, shame, rumination, or comparing yourself to others. Optionally, use the Being a Good Parent to Yourself worksheet in the free tools.

4. Continue to practice having an external, mindful focus whenever you feel anxious around others (including during your homework experiments and other challenging experiences).

CHAPTER 7

Confident Imagery: Using Your Imagination to Change Your Thinking

In the previous chapter we worked with several reframing strategies to verbally challenge and change your distorted hot thoughts that make you feel so much anxiety and shame. You can also do reframing by using imagery rather than words: modifying the shame-based, anxious pictures and impressions in your mind—your "mind's eye"—so that you see yourself handling challenges with self-confidence and pride. That is the focus of this chapter.

Let's first review the progress you've been making in your recent self-therapy homework:

First describe your progress in becoming externally mindful, especially when you're anxious: focusing your attention on the person, conversation, or activity with an attitude of curiosity while treating any thoughts and feelings as background noise. Remember, you don't have direct control over what thoughts and feelings your brain creates. So the goal of external mindfulness is to simply become good at recognizing when thoughts and feelings distract you, and to quickly and gently return your attention to getting engrossed in the conversation, activity, and person in the moment.

_____

_____

_____

_____

What experiments have you done to work on your self-therapy goals? What evidence have you gathered through your experiments related to your hot thoughts and core beliefs? What are you learning about yourself and how others respond to you?

_____

_____

_____

_____

_____

Describe how you've been using the being-a-good-parent-to-yourself strategy, and how it's been helpful.

_____

_____

_____

_____

_____

Have you tried practicing any of the reframing strategies when you've experienced much anxiety, shame, upset, rumination, or avoidance? Which of these strategies are you finding most helpful so far, and in what ways?

_____

_____

_____

_____

_____

Anxious and Shame-Based Images and Impressions

The central principle in cognitive behavioral therapy is that the way we think strongly impacts the way we feel and behave, often fueling vicious cycles that create anxiety and shame and hurt our interactions. You've already begun practicing several strategies aimed at modifying your self-defeating thoughts and behaviors. Another strategy that many socially anxious people find helpful for this purpose is to use imagery to increase self-confidence and pride and to decrease anxiety and shame.

Not all our thoughts come in the form of words. When we're anxious, many of us think primarily in images and impressions. We often "see" ourselves as coming across badly and others reacting badly toward us. For some of us, these images come in the form of vivid mental pictures, like videos in our mind's eye, often brimming with emotion. For others, these thoughts come in the form of impressions: ideas and concerns that may not be visual or verbal, but may still be replete with anxiety and shame. With practice, you can learn to modify your mental images and impressions so that you experience more self-confidence. For many people, this is a powerful reframing strategy that can help you lessen anticipatory anxiety and worry, as well as post-event rumination.

Here are some common anxious and shame-based images and impressions:

- **Appearing extremely anxious:** beet-red blushing, sweating like a pig, shaking like a dog

- **Speaking and performing poorly:** not having anything to say during long and awkward silences, saying something stupid or offensive, voice quivering weirdly

- **Others reacting negatively:** laughing at you, grimacing at you, criticizing you harshly, pointing and looking at you while talking to others

As you can see, mental images and impressions can be quite extreme, often more so than verbal thoughts. They tend to be the most emotionally laden forms of thinking when experiencing anxiety and shame.

Pick a few situations that often strongly trigger your social anxiety and shame. Describe the images or impressions you have then:

Triggering situations:

1. _____

2. _____

3. _____

Images and impressions when feeling anxiety or shame about these situations:

1. _____

2. _____

3. _____

Anxious and shame-based images and impressions not only make you suffer emotionally. Just like verbal hot thoughts, they also lead you to engage in avoidance, self-focused attention, and other safety-seeking behaviors that hurt how you feel, come across, converse, and perform. These negative images and impressions help fuel your vicious cycle of anxiety and shame.

Confident Imagery to Reframe Your Hot Thoughts

With practice, you can learn to change these anxious images and impressions (McEvoy, Saulsman, and Rapee 2017). Imagine a more self-confident version of yourself. Self-confidence doesn't mean you expect everyone to respond positively to you. That would be arrogant and also unrealistic! Self-confidence means believing you can handle challenging situations well, regardless of how others respond. Sure, a more self-confident version of you expects most people to react positively or at least neutrally to you. But the self-confident you would accept the occasional negative reaction as a mere disappointment, not devastation, because you'd see it as simply representing the other person's different preferences or circumstances, not your worth.

Reread your anxious and shame-based images and impressions you wrote above. Now write how you imagine the self-confident version of you would appear and behave in these triggering situations. Include how you'd confidently handle a variety of reactions from others: positive, neutral, ambiguous, and negative. Don't hold back; go for it! Write exactly how you'd like to appear and behave, even if you think that's out of reach for you now.

Read the following instructions for practicing confident imagery before trying this on your own:

- Close your eyes and imagine yourself in a situation that often triggers anxiety and shame. First set the scene in your mind's eye: vividly "see" the place you're in and the people and things that are there. Try to bring additional senses into your imagery to make it more vivid—not only what you see, but also what you hear and perhaps also touch, taste, and smell. If you don't see vivid mental pictures in your mind, try narrating in the present tense what you're observing in the way an author vividly describes a scene in a novel. (For example: "I'm in a large room filled with people who are all conversing in groups of two, three, and four. It's noisy with conversation, laughter, and background music. I grab a soda from the refreshment table, and I feel the glass in my fingers and taste the sweet and bubbly drink as I slowly look around at the people there.") Whether in mental pictures or narration, make sure you're describing *yourself inside that scene in the present*, not watching yourself in that scene at another time, as if in a movie or video.

- Then imagine yourself—whether in imagery or verbal narration—*handling that challenging situation with self-confidence in the present*. (For example: "I slowly walk through the room looking at people and smiling when I make eye contact with them. I walk up to someone who smiles back, and I join the small group that she's conversing in. I listen to what they're saying, looking at whoever is speaking, and I smile, nod and laugh in response. I make a comment or ask a question in reaction to what someone says, then introduce myself to the group.") You may want to repeat a challenging scene within that situation a few times, imagining handling it with greater self-confidence in each repetition. You may then move on to other challenging scenes within that situation to practice handling these with self-confidence, too.

- Also practice visual imagery or narration with *different types of responses from others—positive, neutral, ambiguous, and negative—*so you can experience increasing self-confidence in all these scenarios. (For example: "After a few minutes of attempting to converse in a small group that repeatedly ignores my comments, I say, 'Excuse me' and leave the group. I congratulate myself for being friendly, and I tell myself I don't know why *they* weren't friendly, but it's a reflection of them and not me. I look around and find another group, which I walk up to and join.")

- Important: don't spend time in your imagery or narration scripting what to say, as that's a self-defeating safety-seeking behavior. Just imagine yourself handling the scenes with confidence, regardless of what you say or how others react.

Now, reread the preceding instructions so they are fresh in your mind. Then set this book aside and practice confident imagery a few times. It's okay if you're feeling anxious during this exercise. With further practice, you'll feel increasingly calm and confident. Be patient and encouraging with yourself when doing this exercise—like a good parent—and try to spend at least five minutes practicing.

Self-Therapy Homework Practice

Visit http://www.newharbinger.com/54322 to download the worksheets for this chapter.

1. Following the bulleted instructions in the previous section, practice confident imagery for at least five minutes on at least three days. Practice this before doing your homework experiments. You may also practice before other anxiety or shame-triggering situations.

2. Choose and carry out one or more experiments to work on one of your self-therapy goals. Use the Experiment Worksheet in the free tools before and after your experiments.

3. Continue to practice having an external, mindful, curious focus, especially whenever you feel anxious around others (including during your experiments).

4. Practice being a good parent to yourself for any situation that triggers anxiety, shame, rumination, or comparing yourself to others. Definitely practice after your experiments this week. Optionally, you may use the Being a Good Parent to Yourself Worksheet in the free tools.

5. [OPTIONAL] Practice using one or more of the reframing strategies whenever you feel strong anxiety or shame, are ruminating, or are avoiding. Use the reframing worksheets in the free tools.

CHAPTER 8

Pride and Gratitude: Defeating Your Negativity Bias

So far, we've been working with several cognitive and behavioral strategies to identify, challenge and change your hot thoughts and core beliefs that cause you social anxiety and shame and lead you to engage in self-defeating safety-seeking behaviors. In this chapter, I introduce a proactive strategy aimed at increasing your self-confidence and pride and overcoming your negativity bias that fuels social anxiety and shame.

Let's begin by reviewing the progress you've been making in your self-therapy homework practice:

Describe your experience in practicing confident imagery in advance of doing especially anxiety-provoking experiments. Have you noticed anxiety gradually diminishing and being replaced with increasing self-confidence? Has it helped you follow through on doing the experiments in real life? As with any new skill, continued practice is likely to improve your ability to use confident imagery effectively.

_____

_____

_____

_____

_____

How have your recent experiments been going? What evidence have you been gathering to counter your hot thoughts and underlying core beliefs? What are the key learning points you have gained and strengthened from these experiments?

_____

_____

_____

_____

Describe how your practice of external mindful focus has been going, especially whenever you're anxious.

_____

_____

_____

Have you been practicing the strategy of being a good parent to yourself, ideally after every experiment and other anxiety- or shame-triggering situation? How has this helped?

_____

_____

What reframing strategies have you been using so far, and how you have found them to be helpful?

_____

_____

_____

Remember to not let perfectionism frustrate or demoralize you. Be patient and persistent. These are challenging strategies in which you are changing old thinking and behavior patterns that you've had for most of your life. We'll continue practicing these strategies, and over time they'll become healthy new habits for you.

Seeing the Whole Picture: Overcoming Your Negativity Bias

There is much research showing that socially anxious people have a bias toward focusing their attention and thoughts on the ways they think they may be coming across badly to others, while discounting or not noticing the ways that interactions are going well (Koban et al. 2017). This *negativity bias* helps fuel the vicious cycles that lead to anxiety, shame, and reliance on self-defeating safety-seeking behaviors.

It is certainly not the goal of cognitive behavioral therapy to turn you into a Pollyanna, who sees everything in life as good, as though wearing rose-colored glasses. Instead, CBT helps you to take your dark shades off: to see and appreciate the whole picture, not just what seems to be wrong. And you've already been practicing several of these CBT strategies aimed at overcoming your negativity bias. External mindfulness, experiments to test hot thoughts and core beliefs, being a good parent to yourself, reframing, and confident imagery all help you to see the whole picture of your life in ways that are more realistic, helpful, and compassionate. Keeping a daily Pride and Gratitude Log is another CBT strategy that you can use proactively to help you overcome your negativity bias and to see and appreciate the positive in your life and in yourself.

Keeping a Pride and Gratitude Log

Is this just a gratitude journal you've probably heard so much about? No, the Pride and Gratitude Log, located at the end of the chapter, goes deeper. Since shame (based on core beliefs that there is something fundamentally wrong with you) is at the root of social anxiety disorder for most people, it is important to foster pride (based on the belief that you have many positive qualities) as well as gratitude (appreciating the positive aspects of your life). So I add the key step of identifying your underlying strengths and qualities exemplified by each positive experience you write in order to help foster self-pride.

I also prefer to call this a log, rather than a journal, to lessen any fear and avoidance you may experience about writing. It's effective enough to spend just five minutes or so daily keeping a list of positive experiences and your underlying qualities they exemplify. Keep a simple *list* of brief entries; not a series of essays.

Here are the basic instructions:

- Make it a daily practice to think back over the past twenty-four hours and, in an ongoing log, write down anything positive that you experienced. Don't disqualify the positive, no matter how small, imperfect, or repeated the positive experience is. Be specific in what you write. Don't write any qualifiers or anything negative here. (If you're feeling distressed about something, then separately use one of the reframing strategies described in chapter 6.) And definitely include positive things you did, and positive evidence you observed, during any experiments you conducted that day.

- It doesn't matter whether or not you actually *feel* pride or gratitude at this point. If it's at least partly positive, then write it down! With further practice in regularly using this log, you'll likely begin to actually feel proud and grateful.

- Reenter positive things that occur on more than one day. If you stop including positive things because you've included them in the past, you're implicitly giving yourself the distorted message that they don't count, and you may take them for granted. But do try to include at least one non-routine experience daily. Many people find it helpful to add the step to choose something positive to do in the coming day that you can later enter in your Pride and Gratitude Log!

- Reread your entries for the day, and then write down your strengths or qualities that these positive experiences exemplify. This helps you see that one small positive thing is reflective of a strength or quality of yours that is actually very important and enduring. For example, if you wrote the entry "I had a good conversation with a friend," you could then write, "This is evidence that I can be an engaging conversationalist, a good friend, and a likable person."

- It's important to enter items in the log every day in order to retrain your mind to look for and value these previously neglected positive things about your life and yourself. Some people find it helpful to schedule a regular time every day to complete the log, paired with some activity they are already in the habit of doing daily (e.g., during their first cup of coffee, when eating lunch, or just before going to bed). Perhaps set an electronic alert to remind you.

- Some people prefer to make entries in their log multiple times during the day, soon after experiencing something positive. They find that it's easier to remember these experiences this way, and that it reinforces the positive feelings they get from them more powerfully. If you use this approach, just make sure you make your entries at least once per day.

- Periodically reread your log, or sections of it, especially when you want a mood or confidence boost!

Examples and Practice

Let's practice together making entries into your Pride and Gratitude Log so that you feel more confident doing so as self-therapy homework in the coming week. The first step is to think back over the past twenty-four hours and try to recall all that you experienced that day. Then write down anything positive you experienced, no matter how small and no matter how imperfect it may have been. Include positive evidence generated by any experiments you may have conducted. Here are some examples to help get you in this frame of mind:

- I got out of bed and managed to get to work on time, despite feeling like I wanted to call in sick and stay in bed.

- I got most of my work done today, and did it well enough, despite finding some of it difficult and some of it boring.

- I had a pleasant conversation with my coworker, Sarah, despite feeling anxious about it. I attempted to focus mindfully on the conversation rather than on my anxious thoughts and feelings. I kept the conversation going for ten minutes, rather than ending it early due to anxiety as I usually would.

Now, it's your turn. Write a list of anything positive you experienced, no matter how small or imperfect. Don't let your negativity bias stop you from writing down anything that was in some small way positive:

_____

_____

_____

_____

_____

_____

_____

The next step is to reread your entries and to write down the personal strengths or qualities of yours that they are evidence of. For my list of examples, I might write:

- Commitment to doing a good job at work

- Being a good conversationalist when I focus mindfully

- Being enjoyable company and likable

- Being brave: willing to do some things that make me anxious

- Commitment to taking care of my mental and physical health

Your turn now. Reread your own list of experiences, and write down your strengths and qualities they exemplify. Don't let your negativity bias disqualify the positive. If this is difficult, imagine you're identifying the qualities of someone else who had these experiences:

_____

_____

_____

_____

_____

_____

The last and optional step is to identify at least one positive activity you plan to do the following day, which you'll later be able to enter into your log. For example, you might choose to have longer conversations with coworkers or to invite someone to lunch. What do you choose to do?

_____

_____

_____

Self-Therapy Homework for the Coming Week

Visit http://www.newharbinger.com/54322 to download the worksheets for this chapter.

1. Following the bulleted instructions in this chapter, make entries into a Pride and Gratitude Log every day, including your underlying strengths and qualities these entries represent. Include positive things you did and experienced during experiments. You can use the Pride and Gratitude Log worksheet (below and in the free tools) or keep your log in a notebook, on your computer, or in your phone.

2. Practice using confident imagery before doing your homework experiment(s). You may also practice before other anxiety- or shame-triggering situations as well.

3. Choose and carry out one or more experiments to work on one of your self-therapy goals. Use the Experiment Worksheet in the free tools before and after your experiments.

4. Continue to practice having an external, mindful focus whenever you feel anxious (including during your experiments).

5. Practice being a good parent to yourself for any situation that triggers anxiety, shame, rumination, or comparing yourself to others. Definitely practice after your experiments. Optionally, use the Being a Good Parent to Yourself Worksheet in the free tools.

6. [OPTIONAL] Practice using one or more of the reframing strategies whenever you feel strong anxiety or shame, are ruminating, or are avoiding. Use the reframing worksheets in the free tools.

Pride and Gratitude Log

Date _____

Positive experiences and evidence this past day: _____
_____
_____
_____
_____
_____
_____

Underlying strengths or qualities of yours evidenced by these experiences:
_____
_____
_____
_____

Positive action(s) you plan to do in the coming day, which you'll later be able to enter in this log:
_____
_____
_____
_____

CHAPTER 9

Paradoxical Experiments: Confronting Your Anxiety and Shame

Let's review where we've been and where we're going. Up until now, we've been working on several strategies to break your vicious cycles of social anxiety and shame. You've been learning to test and modify your hot thoughts and core beliefs that are at the root of your problems and to drop your safety-seeking behaviors that were making you feel and do worse. In this chapter, we go further by directly confronting your anxiety and shame through experiments paradoxically designed to make your fears come true so that you can build the self-confidence and pride to know that you can handle no matter what life throws your way. Sounds scary, I know. But we'll approach this in a series of small steps no harder or riskier than you believe you can handle.

Let's first discuss your self-therapy homework:

How has your use of the Pride and Gratitude Log been going and feeling for you? Are you not only listing positive experiences you've had, but also identifying your positive qualities they exemplify? Are you countering any perfectionistic tendencies to disqualify items you consider writing for not being big or perfect enough? Since this log is aimed at changing the negativity bias that fuels your social anxiety and shame, are you making *daily written entries* rather than doing so sporadically or just in your head?

_____

_____

_____

_____

Have you practiced using confident imagery in advance of doing especially anxiety-provoking experiments? Has this helped you feel less anticipatory anxiety and more motivation to follow through on the experiments?

_____

_____

How have your recent experiments been going? What evidence have you been gathering to counter your hot thoughts and underlying core beliefs? What are the key learning points you have gained and strengthened?

_____

_____

_____

How are you doing with practicing and strengthening the skill of external mindful focus whenever you're anxious, including during all your experiments?

_____

_____

Have you continued to practice the strategy of being a good parent to yourself, ideally after each of your experiments and other anxiety- or shame-triggering situations? Has this helped you to overcome self-critical rumination?

_____

_____

Have you tried practicing any of the optional reframing strategies when you experience much anxiety, shame, upset, rumination, or avoidance? Which of these reframing strategies are you finding most helpful so far, and in what ways?

_____

_____

Please don't let perfectionism discourage or overwhelm you. There's no need to be perfect in using these strategies! Continuing to practice them will help you make further progress toward your self-therapy goals.

Paradoxical vs. Straightforward Experiments

The core of this self-therapy work has been conducting experiments to test your hot thoughts and core beliefs that give rise to your social anxiety and shame. All the other strategies are primarily used before, during, or after your experiments so that the experiments may be more helpful learning experiences for you.

Up until now, the experiments you've been doing have been straightforward: you choose to take challenging steps to help you work on your self-therapy goals. If you're working on making friends or dating, for example, your experiments might involve attending meetups or other social activities in which you meet and converse with strangers, and maybe later invite them out. Or if your goals are more career oriented, you may be doing experiments such as speaking up at meetings, networking at work events, giving presentations, or interviewing for jobs. Or maybe you're working on overcoming other anxiety triggers by doing experiments such as interacting with strangers in nonsocial settings, doing things when you may be observed by others, performing in front of a group, asserting your opinions and desires, using public bathrooms, or being sexual.

I'd like to introduce you now to a new type of experiment to add to your repertoire: **paradoxical experiments**, aka decatastrophizing (Clark 2023a), social mishap (Hofmann 2023), and shame-attacking (Ellis 2016) exposures. A paradox is something that seems contradictory or opposed to common sense, but which is true nonetheless. In cognitive behavioral therapy for social anxiety, *a paradoxical experiment is one in which you attempt to make a fear come true in order to overcome that fear*. That probably seems contradictory and contrary to common sense; wouldn't having a fear materialize only make you more afraid the next time? But, paradoxically, if *you seek out your fears on purpose*, you'll learn something that actually makes you less afraid: either that your fears rarely come true or, if they do, that they aren't nearly as big a deal as you had thought they were, and that you can handle them much better than you had imagined. Your fears are "decatastrophized." Over time, conducting paradoxical experiments will help you diminish your anxiety and shame and build self-confidence and pride.

The objective is to evoke your fears in order to test them out. So, for example, if you fear saying something stupid or foolish, you might ask a dumb question on purpose, or say something obviously incorrect. If your fear is appearing anxious to others, you might make yourself appear to blush, sweat, or jitter on purpose when interacting with someone. If you fear rejection, seek out rejection by asking people things they are likely to turn you down for. If you fear performing badly, make a mistake on purpose that others can observe.

All this may seem a bit bizarre and awfully scary. But by taking it in small steps, paradoxical experiments won't be any harder or riskier than you feel ready to handle. And, paradoxically, this type of experiment tends to become rather fun and funny over time, as you see that other people don't even notice—or don't seem to care—about your blunders.

The types of paradoxical experiments you could do are endless; here are many examples:

Examples of Paradoxical Experiments

- Make mistakes or do a mediocre job on purpose (e.g., at work tasks, in emails or messages, speaking in meetings, when hosting a meal or social activity), as long as you don't harm others.

- Ask someone's name after they had already told you earlier.

- Say "It's so good to see you after so long, Steve/Sally!" to someone you don't know.

- Exaggerate or create your anxiety symptoms on purpose when you interact with people (e.g., sweating, blushing, jitteriness, voice quivering). For example, you could do vigorous exercise, rub your cheeks, wear too much blush, or put water on your face or clothes before talking to someone.

- During conversations, create a pause, deliberately mispronounce a word, say something incorrect or foolish, or try to be uninteresting.

- Ask for something you know the restaurant doesn't serve or the store doesn't have.

- Answer a question incorrectly, or ask something already answered, in a class or meeting.

- Have brief conversations with strangers and ask them out, with the goal of being rejected by multiple people.

- Ask "stupid questions" on purpose (e.g., directions to an obvious location or a product you're standing right by).

- Order a coffee; when the server gives it to you, ask if it's decaf, and then unapologetically say you want decaf.

- Bring items to a checkout line. After they're rung up, unapologetically say you don't have enough money and ask to buy it for less.

- Go to a restaurant or bar and order only tap water; drink the water, thank the server, and leave without apology.

- Go to a store, ask for assistance to find an item, then buy it. Immediately return the item, unapologetically saying that you changed your mind.

- Draw attention to yourself in public settings by acting foolish (e.g., singing or dancing strangely, walking backward, calling out the names of train/bus/elevator stops).

- Sing poorly at karaoke or perform poorly at an open mic night.

- Ask for extra-small condoms at a drug store.

- Ask multiple people if they can spare you ten dollars because you're running low.

- Do an activity in public that you're not good at (e.g., juggling, singing, playing guitar), and put out a hat for donations.

- Walk around strangers with toilet paper hanging out the back of your pants.

- Dress poorly, wear obviously unmatched or inside-out clothes, or have very visible stains on your clothing while at work or a social activity.

- Attend a meeting of an organization and express an opinion that is contrary to the organization's norm.

- Express contrary opinions with individuals (e.g., about restaurants, movies, politics, religion) when you actually don't care.

- Interrupt people occasionally during conversations.

- Ask strangers for help or for favors you do not need, or ask to have their pictures taken with you, with the goal of collecting rejections.

- Drop change or spill a drink where strangers will see you.

- Tell people unapologetically that you're anxious, even when you're not (e.g., in conversations, meetings, radio call-ins).

Paradoxical Experiments to Confront Your Own Fears

Now it's your turn to identify paradoxical experiments you could do to help you overcome your social anxiety and shame. Complete the following worksheet (also available in the free tools at http://www.newharbinger.com/54322). Make sure to include things that don't feel too difficult for you to do right away, but also include things you'd like to be able to do in the future as you build further self-confidence through this program.

My Paradoxical Experiments Worksheet

My major feared outcomes (not the situations that trigger your anxiety, but what you fear could happen in those situations):

___

___

___

___

___

___

Paradoxical experiment ideas to evoke these fears:

___

___

___

___

___

___

___

___

___

___

___

___

Strategies for Doing Paradoxical Experiments

Does the idea of doing paradoxical experiments feel too scary for you? Here are some ideas that may help:

- Consider asking a good friend to do paradoxical experiments with you. Even if someone isn't usually socially anxious, everyone has some social fears, and your friend might enjoy the experience of doing some challenging experiments together. You can approach it as a game and have fun with it! Taking turns doing these experiments side by side—or in some cases doing joint experiments—will likely embolden both of you to go further than you would on your own.

- You can approach your experiments hierarchically. This isn't macho therapy! If one idea you have feels too scary to do now, think of an easier version of that same experiment to do at first, or do a different experiment to challenge that same fear. As you practice, you'll build self-confidence and will feel ready to do even more challenging experiments later.

- Try doing reframing (chapter 6) or using confident imagery (chapter 7) about your paradoxical experiment before you carry it out. This will help reduce your anticipatory anxiety and increase your motivation.

- You may want to do some experiments that are purely paradoxical, such as asking a series of people at a grocery store where the milk is when you're standing right by it. The advantage of this strategy is that you can gather a lot of evidence from multiple people in a short time. However, you may sometimes find it more beneficial to do a brief paradoxical experiment embedded within a longer straightforward experiment. For example, you could make conversation with a stranger at a social activity, ask for their name a second time even though you had already asked earlier, and then continue the conversation. The advantage of embedding a paradoxical experiment in a longer straightforward experiment is that you not only see the person's immediate reaction, but you also observe whether the (intentional) social blunder has any impact on the remainder of the interaction.

Self-Therapy Homework Practice

Visit http://www.newharbinger.com/54322 to download the worksheets for this chapter.

1. Choose and carry out one or more paradoxical experiments to work on your self-therapy goals. You may also want to do a straightforward experiment, or embed a paradoxical experiment within your straightforward experiment. Use the Experiment Worksheet in the free tools before and after your experiment(s).

2. [OPTIONAL] Practice using confident imagery before your experiment(s) or for other anxiety- or shame-triggering situations.

3. [OPTIONAL] Before your experiment(s), or on any day you're bothered by anxiety, shame, upset, rumination, or avoidance for at least an hour, use one or more of the reframing strategies. Use the reframing worksheets in the free tools.

4. Continue making daily entries into your Pride and Gratitude Log, including your underlying qualities the entries represent. Include positive evidence you gathered during experiments. Use the Pride and Gratitude Log worksheet in the free tools, or keep your log in a notebook, on your computer, or in your phone.

5. Continue to practice having an external, mindful focus whenever you feel anxious around others (including during your homework experiments).

6. [OPTIONAL] Practice being a good parent to yourself for any situation that triggers anxiety, shame, rumination, or comparing yourself to others. Also use this strategy after your experiments. Optionally, you may use the Being a Good Parent to Yourself Worksheet in the free tools.

CHAPTER 10

Head-Held-High Assertion: Standing Up for Yourself

Several of the cognitive and behavioral strategies you've been practicing so far in this self-therapy program are aimed in part at testing and changing your anxious hot thoughts: your feared predictions of how things may turn out. But what if your fears sometimes come true? In this chapter I discuss the use of assertiveness to help build self-confidence, lessen anxiety and shame about your fears coming true, and affirm your personal dignity.

Let's first review the progress you've been making in practicing the CBT strategies:

Have you done paradoxical experiments, perhaps in addition to, or embedded within, straightforward experiments? How have you worked up the courage to confront your fears? Have you seen that it's hard to make your fears come true, or if they did, that they weren't as big a deal as you had thought they'd be? What evidence have you been gathering to counter your hot thoughts and underlying core beliefs?

_____

_____

_____

_____

_____

_____

Have you practiced using confident imagery in advance of doing especially anxiety-provoking experiments? Has this helped lessen your anticipatory anxiety and increase your motivation to do your experiments?

_____

_____

Have you practiced any of the optional reframing strategies when you're experiencing much anxiety, shame, upset, rumination, or avoidance? Which of these reframing strategies are you finding most helpful so far, and in what ways?

_____

_____

How has your use of the Pride and Gratitude Log been going and feeling for you? Has this begun to improve your mood and self-confidence?

_____

_____

How are you doing with utilizing the skill of external mindful focus whenever you're anxious, including during all your experiments?

_____

_____

Have you practiced the strategy of being a good parent to yourself, especially after experiments and other anxiety- or shame-triggering situations? Has this helped you to overcome self-critical rumination?

_____

_____

Remember to be patient and persevere. Continuing to practice these strategies will turn them into healthy habits and will help you make further progress.

The Power of Assertion

Social anxiety is *not* an irrational fear. The things you're anxious about—judgment, criticism, rejection, embarrassment—indeed do happen from time to time in everyone's life! The strategy of doing paradoxical experiments is aimed at helping you see that your fears don't come true as often as you expect, and if they do, that they aren't as bad as you imagined. Practicing being assertive in the face of fears that come true will help you further build self-confidence that you can handle whatever life throws your way with a sense of pride rather than shame.

There are actually two uses of assertion in cognitive behavioral therapy for social anxiety:

- **Assertion as a self-therapy goal:** If you have social anxiety about asserting your opinions and feelings—at least about some topics, in some situations, or with some people—then doing experiments in which your goal is to honestly and respectfully express your desires or ideas would help you make progress. For example, you may want to do assertiveness experiments in which you honestly tell a friend what restaurant you want to go to; ask a service provider to correct a problem; state a contrary opinion about a political, religious, or work-related issue; or tell someone you're close to that you are upset at something they said or did.

- **Assertion as a strategy to decrease anticipatory anxiety and post-event shame:** Learning to assert yourself with your head held high—with a sense of dignity and pride rather than defensiveness or shame—will increase your self-confidence that you can cope well whenever your fears come true (aka "assertive defense of the self"; Padesky 1997). For example, if you fear being criticized, think how it would feel to tell the critic something like "I respect your right to your opinion, but I see things differently." Or if you dread saying something stupid, imagine responding to your gaffe like this: "Oops, that was a silly thing to say! I guess we all goof from time to time!" Or if someone comments that you seem anxious, consider calmly asserting: "I do get a bit nervous talking to new people, but I'm enjoying our conversation."

Whether expressing your feelings or opinions or standing up for yourself in the face of fears that have come true, *assertion is self-affirming because it acts on the belief that you matter as much as others.* Assertion may not result in the change you desire from other people, but it does affirm your dignity and worth and decrease your anxiety and shame.

Asserting Your Opinions and Feelings

With what topics, situations, or people do you tend to avoid asserting your opinions or feelings due to anticipatory anxiety?

_____
_____
_____
_____

What are your hot thoughts or fears about asserting yourself then?

_____
_____
_____
_____

Let's use the reframing strategy of *true-however-therefore* to make your hot thoughts more realistic, helpful, and self-compassionate. For example, you might say: "It's *true* that Sean has a different opinion than I. *However*, if I express my own opinion without putting him down, he's likely to respect me for doing so. It may even improve our friendship because he'll know me better. If he reacts badly, that would reflect badly on him, not me. *Therefore*, I'll tell Sean that I respect his opinion, but then state directly what I believe." Now try using this *true-however-therefore* reframing strategy to challenge your own hot thoughts about asserting your opinions or feelings:

_____
_____
_____
_____
_____

Here are a few important pointers to keep in mind when considering asserting yourself:

Assert your opinion or feelings in a way that is respectful of the other person and doesn't put them down or label them. Express yourself calmly, not angrily. But do express yourself directly, without apology, qualifications, fake excuses, or indirect hints, which are safety-seeking behaviors that hurt how you feel and come across. For example, say: "I have a different opinion. I believe that…" as opposed to "You're wrong! Don't you think that…?" Or "I was annoyed when you arrived so late, because it left me wondering if you respected my feelings" as opposed to "I can't believe how inconsiderate you are!" Or "I don't like that restaurant so much. I'd prefer we go to…" as opposed to "I'm sorry, would you mind if we tried something else? I just went there the other day [which isn't true]." If you express yourself indirectly, timidly, apologetically, angrily, or insultingly, the other person is less likely to respect your message, and you may degrade your own self-respect!

Although I believe that scripting what to say in a social conversation is a self-defeating safety-seeking behavior, I do believe that scripting and practicing brief assertions ahead of time will help you feel more confident about handling this sensitive challenge in a manner you can feel proud about, regardless of the other person's response. Write examples of how you would you like to assert yourself—respectfully, calmly, and directly—in the situations you identified above:

_____

_____

_____

_____

_____

_____

_____

_____

_____

Weigh the risks and benefits of asserting yourself in a particular circumstance. Most of the time, the only risk is that you may not get your way, but there are usually no lasting costs. Even so, the potential benefits of assertion include increased self-confidence and closer relationships. Using reframing (true-however-therefore) will help you determine whether the risks you perceive are realistic or distorted. Sometimes assertion could lead to hurting others or ourselves, with little benefit. For example, I would assert my tastes in music and restaurants to a friend who disagrees, but I wouldn't tell that friend that I didn't like the food they made for me! Or, I would assert myself with my boss about needing guidance on a project, but I wouldn't tell my boss that I think they're doing a poor job in managing our team. Weigh the risks and benefits of asserting yourself in the examples you described above:

Risks: _____

_____

_____

Benefits: _____

_____

_____

Head-Held-High Assertions When Fears Come True

Assertion can also be used as a strategy to decrease your anxiety about the possibility of interactions going badly for you. Becoming confident that you can handle your fears coming true—with dignity, through assertive and respectful comments and actions—will help you decrease your anxiety and shame. Review the examples of fears coming true and head-held-high assertions on the following worksheet and notice how you relate:

Head-Held-High Assertion Worksheet
(Example)

Fears Come True	Head-Held-High Assertions
I start blushing/sweating/jittering when mingling with new people at a social event, and someone tells me I look weird and weak.	"I do sometimes get nervous when talking to new people, but I'm enjoying our conversation. We all have quirks." [Then continue the conversation.]
I say something stupid or incorrect during a conversation, and the other person gives me a weird look. I assume they think poorly of me and have lost respect for me.	"That was a silly thing for me to say. Oh well! We all do that at times." [Then continue the conversation.]
There's a long, awkward pause when conversing with a new person.	"Ooh, it looks like that topic sure ran dry!" [Then ask a curious, open-ended question about something else.]
I unintentionally offend someone in a conversation, and they tell me how hurt or angry they are.	"I apologize. I certainly didn't mean to offend you. I sometime make mistakes, as we all do." [Then continue the conversation.]
Someone tells me that they think I'm boring, unappealing, or unattractive, and rejects me.	"Oh, well. We all have different tastes. Fortunately, other people like me as I am." [Then move on and start a conversation with someone else.]
I appear nervous when speaking at a meeting and someone tells me that must mean I don't know what I'm talking about and am not good at my job.	"It's true that I get nervous speaking in front of groups. Lots of people do. But I happen to be very good at my job and have important things to say." [Then continue speaking at the meeting.]
I go blank when speaking at a meeting because I get distracted. I can't continue speaking, and people start looking at me strangely. I presume they're thinking poorly of me and no longer respect me.	"Excuse me. I'm afraid I just lost track of what I was saying. Oh, well. I'll go back to my previous point and continue from there. I'd appreciate your patience and attention." [Then continue speaking at the meeting.]

Now, it's your turn. Identify the things you're most afraid of happening when you're feeling socially anxious, even if you think it's unlikely, and write these in the Fears Come True column. For each fear, write what you would want to *say* and *do* in response that feels dignified to you, even if you think you wouldn't have the nerve to actually follow through. (We'll work on building your courage soon!) Stand up for yourself. Make sure your comments are not defensive, overly apologetic, or indirect. And be calm and respectful in what you say; avoid labeling the other person, putting them down, or expressing strong anger, as that makes you come across as mean or out of control and may lead you to feel worse later. Complete the following worksheet, also available to download at http://www.newharbinger.com/54322.

Head-Held-High Assertion Worksheet

Fears Come True	Head-Held-High Assertions (what you would SAY and DO in response; be calm, direct, and respectful, not defensive or apologetic)

Building Your Courage to Assert Yourself

As much as you may like the idea of being more assertive—whether to express your feelings or opinions or to stand up for yourself when your fears materialize—you may feel too scared to do so. I suggest you use these CBT strategies to build your courage. Remember, courage doesn't mean having no fear. To the contrary, courage means doing something important to you (e.g., asserting yourself) *despite feeling afraid*. Try using these strategies before asserting yourself:

- **Reframing:** Challenge your hot thoughts about asserting yourself in a situation that makes you anxious by using one of the reframing strategies, such as true-however-therefore (chapter 6).

- **Confident imagery:** Use your imagination (in pictures or narration) to practice asserting yourself confidently in situations when you're anxious (chapter 7). Repeat your imagery until you feel confident asserting yourself.

- **Role-plays:** If you're seeing a therapist, or have a trusted friend, try practicing asserting yourself with your therapist or friend playing the role of the other person in a situation in which you're anxious. Repeat your role-plays until you feel confident in asserting yourself. Watch the clinical demonstration video I made about doing this type of role play, linked in the free tools: Resources at http://www.newharbinger.com/54322.

- **Take it hierarchically:** If, after using the above strategies, asserting yourself in a particular circumstance still feels too scary, choose a less risky situation in which you can assert yourself. You'll likely build courage as you gain positive evidence and experience in these less scary assertions, which will empower you to assert yourself in scarier circumstances.

Combining Assertions with Paradoxical Experiments

Besides feeling anxious, the hardest part of asserting yourself in the face of fears coming true is finding the right opportunities to practice this strategy in real life. If one of your fears does materialize, you may be caught off guard and miss the brief opportunity to assert yourself. To practice, you can create as many opportunities as you want by doing paradoxical experiments designed to make your fears come true, immediately followed by using head-held-high assertions you planned in advance. Using any of the above four CBT strategies will help you build up the courage to do paradoxical experiments capped with head-held-high assertions.

For example, you can ask someone for directions to something obvious that is right there, immediately followed by asserting yourself by saying, "Oops, I can be oblivious at times! We all have our quirks, don't we!" Or, when talking with a stranger with whom you're purposely appearing anxious, you can at some point interject an assertion, such as, "Don't mind me. I get nervous talking to new people, but I'm enjoying our conversation."

Doing multiple paradoxical experiments capped with head-held-high assertions will help you gather a lot of evidence that your fears are not devastating, and that you can handle them with dignity. This will increase your self-confidence and pride, and lessen your anxiety and shame.

Confronting Prejudice

Remember that social anxiety is *not* an irrational fear. Judgment, criticism, rejection, and embarrassment are experiences we all have in our lives. But some people face such experiences more often due to widespread prejudice: preconceived judgments—sometimes accompanied by discriminatory speech and action—based not on individual behavior but on negative beliefs toward certain groups of people. Most every individual has their own prejudices, of course. But so do societies at large, or large segments of societies. Common groups of people who experience societal prejudice include:

- Racial, ethnic, and religious minorities
- Lesbian, gay, bi, trans, and other queer people (LGBTQ+)
- Women
- Young or elderly people
- Immigrants, refugees, and asylum seekers, especially those who are non-white
- People with different political or religious beliefs
- Impoverished people
- Physically and mentally disabled people
- Neurodivergent people
- People who have larger bodies
- People viewed as unattractive
- Introverted people

Below are some ways to apply the cognitive behavioral skills and strategies you've been learning and practicing when faced with societal or individual prejudice. You may want to incorporate some of these strategies into the self-therapy homework you pursue in the coming weeks.

Head-held-high assertions: First write out assertions you would like to use when confronted with individual or societal prejudice. Then, as described above, use *reframing, confident imagery,* and/or *role-plays* to prepare you and build courage. Remember to take it hierarchically: you may feel more ready to assert yourself with some prejudicial people and situations than with others. You may determine that some situations are too risky to do anything more assertive than walking away with your head held high.

Here are some examples of head-held-high assertions in the face of prejudice.

When facing personal prejudice or rejection:

- "Well, everyone has their own tastes!"
- "Okay. I'm an acquired taste!"
- "Oh well. To each their own!"
- "There's no accounting for taste!"
- "That's fine. I wish you well, anyway."

When facing societal prejudice:

- "I see things differently than you."
- "I believe in viewing people as individuals, not stereotypes."
- "I believe prejudice is wrong."
- "You're overgeneralizing. There are people in *all* groups who do bad things!"
- "I believe all people have equal worth and should be treated with respect."

Now, it's your turn. Think of situations in which you fear confronting individual or societal prejudice, and write head-held-high assertions you would like to be able to use then.

_____

_____

_____

_____

_____

_____

_____

_____

Assertive action: Consider what you can do when confronting societal prejudice, such as attend a rally or march, volunteer in a social change organization, write letters of protest or advocacy to public officials or in publications, testify or speak up in a public hearing, or file a complaint. Consider doing one such assertive action as one of your experiments in the coming weeks.

Reframing: Even when you believe it's too risky to assert yourself, or you missed the opportunity to do so, it's important to challenge any rumination that may trouble you after experiencing an act of prejudice. Use the reframing strategies to help you see the prejudicial comment or action as reflecting the other person—their biases, fears, or personal problems and characteristics—and not a judgment of your worth or likability to others.

Check out the blog articles and testimonials (video, audio, and written) about socially anxious people confronting prejudice in the free tools: Resources at http://www.newharbinger.com/54322.

Self-Therapy Homework Practice

Visit http://www.newharbinger.com/54322 to download the worksheets and other materials for this chapter.

1. Choose and carry out one or more paradoxical experiments to work on your self-therapy goals, immediately followed by making a preplanned head-held-high assertion. You may also want to do a straightforward experiment, such as asserting your opinions or feelings, or embed a paradoxical experiment within a straightforward experiment. Consider using a preplanned assertion in the face of prejudice, or doing an assertive action to confront prejudice, as described above. Use the Experiment Worksheet in the free tools before and after your experiment(s).

2. [OPTIONAL] Practice using confident imagery of being assertive in the situations you chose as experiment(s) before doing so in real life.

3. [OPTIONAL] Before your experiment(s), or on any day you're bothered by anxiety, shame, upset, rumination, or avoidance for at least an hour, use one or more of the reframing strategies. Use the reframing worksheets in the free tools.

4. Make daily entries into your Pride and Gratitude Log, including your underlying qualities they represent. Include positive evidence you gathered during experiments.

5. Continue to practice having an external, mindful focus whenever you're anxious around others (including during your homework experiments).

6. [OPTIONAL] Practice being a good parent to yourself for any situation that triggers anxiety, shame, rumination, or comparing yourself to others. Also use this strategy after your experiments. Optionally, you may use the Being a Good Parent to Yourself Worksheet in the free tools.

CHAPTER 11

Going Deeper: Identifying and Changing Your Shame-Based Core Beliefs

From the start of this self-therapy program, we've discussed how core beliefs are the underlying attitudes that shape the way you see yourself and your interactions, generate hot thoughts and safety-seeking behaviors, create anxiety and shame, and thereby reinforce your core beliefs. Our focus so far has primarily been on practicing cognitive and behavioral skills and strategies aimed at breaking this vicious cycle at the surface: testing, challenging, and changing your hot thoughts and safety-seeking behaviors. Many CBT programs for social anxiety stop here, as these skills and strategies alone provide much relief. But *it's the underlying core beliefs that generate the shame that is the heart of social anxiety disorder for most sufferers*, and that differentiates it from all other phobias. In this chapter, we begin to focus our strategy on changing these shame-based core beliefs.

Let's first review the progress you've been making through your homework practice:

Have you done paradoxical experiments (perhaps in addition to, or embedded within, straightforward experiments), followed immediately by using head-held-high assertions? How has this strategy been going and feeling for you? What evidence have you gathered, and what have you learned?

_____

_____

_____

_____

How has practicing using confident imagery before these experiments and assertions helped you?

_____

_____

Have you practiced any of the reframing strategies in advance of these experiments and assertions, or when experiencing a lot of anxiety, shame, upset, rumination, or avoidance? Which of these strategies are you finding most helpful?

_____

_____

In what ways has utilizing the Pride and Gratitude Log benefited you?

_____

_____

How well have you been able to maintain an external mindful focus whenever you're anxious?

_____

_____

How has practicing the being-a-good-parent-to-yourself strategy helped you to overcome self-critical rumination after experiments or other anxiety triggers?

_____

_____

By now, I bet you've found some of these strategies to be more helpful than others. Focus on those going forward. But also practice those that you've used very little or not at all so far, as you may discover that they also help you make progress. If you're feeling overwhelmed by what you've been working on so far, I suggest you delay tackling this new chapter, and instead continue doing the self-therapy homework practice from chapter 10 for another week or more. There's no hurry!

Your Shame-Based Core Beliefs

Remember that core beliefs are the underlying attitudes you have about yourself, other people, and the world. Everyone has core beliefs, which we first develop in childhood. They're our way of making sense of the complexities of all that we experience. Some core beliefs are largely beneficial to us as we live our lives. Other beliefs may help us in some short-term ways—mainly providing a sense of self-protection—but in the long run end up causing bigger and more lasting problems, such as social anxiety, shame, and difficulty pursuing personal priorities.

As we discussed back in chapter 2, core beliefs come in different forms and levels. At their deepest are **absolute beliefs** about yourself, about people in general, and about the way the world is or should be. **Conditional beliefs** (which are typically generated from your absolute beliefs) are if-then ideas you have about yourself, other people, and the world.

Although the specific core beliefs of people suffering from social anxiety and shame may differ widely, these attitudes most commonly fall into the following four related themes:

- **Deficiency**: beliefs that you're not good enough, that there is something fundamentally wrong with you

- **Personalization:** beliefs that negative judgment or rejection by others is a reflection of your fundamental personal deficiency

- **Perfectionism:** beliefs that any deficit in your performance or appearance will lead to judgment and rejection and is a sign of your fundamental personal deficiency

- **Suspiciousness:** beliefs that other people—or certain categories of people—cannot be trusted, and will take advantage of your deficiencies and hurt you if given the chance

Take the time to reread your core beliefs you first identified in chapter 2 (see "Core Beliefs: Your Bad Attitudes") and in every Experiment Worksheet you've completed, beginning in chapter 4. Then read the following example of shame-based core beliefs. I suggest you also read the examples of old and new core beliefs written by former clients of mine who gave me permission to share theirs, available in the free tools: Resources at http://www.newharbinger.com/54322.

Examples of Shame-Based Old Core Beliefs

- I'm different and don't fit in. (absolute belief, deficiency)

- I have poor social skills, and I'm bad at meeting people and connecting well with them. (absolute belief, deficiency)

- If I don't meet others' expectations completely, they won't like or respect me. (conditional belief, perfectionism)

- I should never hurt other people's feelings. (absolute belief, perfectionism)

- Rejection, criticism or judgment means I'm not good enough to be liked or respected. (absolute belief, personalization)

- If I appear or act anxious, people will think I'm weird, weak, or incompetent. (conditional belief, perfectionism, personalization)

- If I let people know the real me, they'll dislike me. (conditional belief, deficiency)

- People will hurt me if I let my guard down. (conditional belief, suspiciousness)

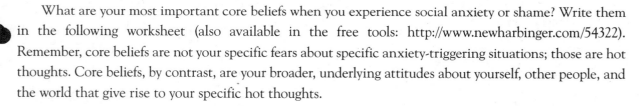

What are your most important core beliefs when you experience social anxiety or shame? Write them in the following worksheet (also available in the free tools: http://www.newharbinger.com/54322). Remember, core beliefs are not your specific fears about specific anxiety-triggering situations; those are hot thoughts. Core beliefs, by contrast, are your broader, underlying attitudes about yourself, other people, and the world that give rise to your specific hot thoughts.

Shame-Based Old Core Beliefs Worksheet

Absolute core beliefs about yourself, other people, or the way the world is or should be:

1. _____
2. _____
3. _____
4. _____

Conditional (if-then) core beliefs about yourself, other people, or the world:

1. _____
2. _____
3. _____
4. _____

Writing Pride-Based Core Beliefs

The next step to changing your shame-based core beliefs is writing a *first draft* of alternative pride-based beliefs. But remember, CBT is not the power of positive thinking. Writing saccharin-sweet beliefs that you simply don't believe won't help; they'll just make you cringe, or even backfire and make you feel worse if you think they apply to others and not to you. These are the criteria to meet when writing your draft of pride-based beliefs:

1. Make sure your new beliefs counter or respond to all your old beliefs.

2. Make sure your new beliefs are *believable* to you (i.e., you consider them to be *probably* true, or you believe them at your best of times).

3. Word your new beliefs in the positive, and avoid double negatives or defensive wording (e.g., "I'm likable and attractive to some people I like," as opposed to "I'm not as unlikable and unattractive as I think"). However, don't write beliefs that are so positive that you don't believe them (e.g., "I'm likable and attractive to anyone I like").

Now consider the following suggestions on how to counter the themes of your shame-based core beliefs:

Deficiency: Consider the reality that everyone has deficiencies as well as strengths. Certainly the people you like are deficient in some ways, but you like these people anyway. Besides, different people have different standards as to what deficiencies and strengths matter to them.

Example: "I have strengths and weaknesses like everyone does. Some people like me despite my weaknesses, just as I like some others despite theirs."

Personalization: Consider the reality that judgment and rejection, however disappointing, reflect the tastes, priorities, and circumstances of the other person and are not a reflection of your personal worth. Different people have different tastes, priorities, and circumstances, so they respond to you differently. *Rejection is a judgment of the match, not of yourself.* If it were your worth or likability as a person that was being judged, then everyone would judge you negatively.

Example: "Because everyone is different, no one can please everyone all of the time. I don't like everyone, and I can't expect everyone to like me."

Perfectionism: Consider the reality that everyone you like performs or appears imperfectly at times. You know that, but you like them anyway. Presumably there are some people who have seen you perform or appear imperfectly but like you nonetheless.

Example: "Everyone is imperfect. Most people don't expect me to be. If someone does, that reflects on them, not me."

Suspiciousness: Consider the reality that some people you know seem to be more trustworthy than others. Also, some people are trustworthy in some ways, but not in other ways. Maybe it's best to determine the trustworthiness of others through small experiments, rather than assume they aren't trustworthy from the outset.

Example: "Most people are trustworthy in some ways and not in others, just like me. I can determine through experience in what ways I can trust someone or not."

Read the example of pride-based core beliefs below. I also encourage you to read the examples of old and new beliefs written by former clients of mine who gave me permission to share their work, available in the free tools: Resources at http://www.newharbinger.com/54322.

Pride-Based New Core Beliefs

- I have commonalities and differences with everyone, as do all people. If someone doesn't respect my differences, it just means they aren't a good match for me.

- I converse and connect well with most people, so long as I focus mindfully and drop other safety-seeking behaviors.

- People like and respect me for who I am, flaws and all, just as I like and respect others despite their imperfections.

- My feelings are as important as anyone's. Although it's usually best to avoid hurting someone's feelings, sometimes it's necessary to risk doing so in order to be honest and true to my needs.

- Rejection just means the other person has different preferences or circumstances. It says nothing about my worth.

- Most people don't notice my anxiety, and if they do, most people don't care. If someone judges me for that, it just means they aren't a good match for me.

- I don't have to be perfect. Just be myself; that's good enough.

It's your turn now. Write your own first draft of pride-based core beliefs that *meet the above three criteria* in the worksheet that follows (also available in the free tools: http://www.newharbinger.com/54322). Don't be perfectionistic; this is just a first draft, and you'll have plenty of opportunity to improve upon these as you make further progress in this program. Rate each new belief for how strongly you believe it now, from 0–100% (51% is a good-enough starting point; you'll be able to strengthen your belief as you make further progress).

Pride-Based New Core Beliefs Worksheet
(Absolute and Conditional)

1. _____
   _____
   _____ Degree of belief: _____%

2. _____
   _____
   _____ Degree of belief: _____%

3. _____
   _____
   _____ Degree of belief: _____%

4. _____
   _____
   _____ Degree of belief: _____%

5. _____
   _____
   _____ Degree of belief: _____%

Affirming Your Pride-Based Core Beliefs

Now that you've written a draft of pride-based core beliefs, I'll guide you in a variety of cognitive behavioral skills and strategies to strengthen these, while weakening your shame-based attitudes. The simplest and most basic of these strategies is to affirm your new core beliefs daily by reciting them out loud, with a tone of conviction, or by listening to a recording of yourself reciting them.

Sounds a little corny? Think about it: you've been frequently affirming your shame-based beliefs thousands of times throughout most of your life via your harshly self-critical, emotionally laden thoughts.

Affirming your new pride-based core beliefs daily will not delete the old neural pathways embedding your old attitudes and feelings. But doing so, along with our other CBT strategies, will help strengthen newer neural pathways embedding feelings of pride and self-confidence.

Let's begin now. Write your pride-based core beliefs on your phone (e.g., in the memo or notes app) so you always have them with you. Then record yourself on your phone reciting your new core beliefs *with a tone of conviction: like you really mean it!* Rerecord yourself repeatedly until you feel strong and confident when reciting them. If something rubs you the wrong way after a few tries, reword it so that it feels truer to you. Then repeat this reciting and recording process until you feel confident. You'll then use this final recording, or real-time reciting of your pride-based beliefs, both proactively (as a routine daily practice) and reactively (when feeling anxiety or shame) in your self-therapy homework practice going forward.

Core Belief Flash Cards

Another core belief change strategy is to write and recite flash cards on which you identify the triggers that activate your shame-based beliefs, and then indicate how you will choose to respond differently going forward. Start by identifying your major triggers for your old core beliefs: not specific instances, but the *types* of situations or interactions that trigger your social anxiety or shame.

_____

_____

_____

_____

Taking one trigger at a time, write a one-paragraph self-statement in which you briefly answer the following questions:

1. What shame-based core belief is activated when you experience this trigger?
2. How does this make you feel and behave in reaction?
3. How is this reaction unhelpful?
4. What is your alternative, pride-based belief to use then?
5. What is a more helpful way to react?

Here is an example of one such flash card:

Potential or Actual Rejection: This triggers my old core belief that I need others' approval to be okay. That belief makes me feel anxious or ashamed, and leads me to be withdrawn and self-conscious around new people. This behavior makes it very hard for others to connect with me, which only leads me to feel worse about myself and ruminate. I now believe that the only approval I actually need is my own. If someone rejects me, it just means that we aren't a good match for each other. I'll take small risks in trying to connect with new people while focusing mindfully. If someone turns out to be a bad fit, I'll pat myself on my back for being friendly and brave, and will move on to talk with someone else.

Now, pick your most important trigger and write a paragraph on your own flash card answering the five questions above:

_____
_____
_____
_____
_____
_____
_____
_____
_____

Write what you put on your flash card on your phone—or take a picture of it—so you can read it whenever you anticipate the triggering situation. You can also write additional flash cards about other triggers.

Self-Therapy Homework Practice

Visit http://www.newharbinger.com/54322 to download the worksheets and other materials for this chapter.

1. Core belief change work:

    a. At least once daily, recite your pride-based core beliefs out loud with a tone of conviction, or listen to your recording. Do so proactively at a routine time, ideally early every day (e.g., during your first cup of coffee), so that it's fresh in your mind throughout the day. Also do so reactively whenever you're alone and feeling social anxiety or shame and perhaps ruminating. Then focus mindfully on a valued activity. Optionally, you may make changes in your pride-based beliefs whenever you have ideas as to how to make them resonate more.

    b. Read your flash card, ideally out loud, whenever you anticipate experiencing the triggering situation. Optionally, you may write additional flash cards on other triggers and put these on your phone to read as needed.

2. Choose and carry out one or more paradoxical experiments to work on your self-therapy goals, immediately followed by making a preplanned head-held-high assertion. You may also want to do a straightforward experiment, such as asserting your opinions or feelings, or embed a paradoxical experiment within a straightforward experiment. Use the Experiment Worksheet in the free tools before and after your experiment(s).

3. Make daily entries into your Pride and Gratitude Log, including your underlying qualities these represent. Include positive evidence you gathered during experiments.

4. Continue to practice having an external, mindful focus during your homework experiments and whenever you're anxious around others.

5. [OPTIONAL] Practice any of the following strategies that you find helpful or that you haven't tried enough to determine how helpful it is.

    a. Practice using confident imagery of conducting your experiment and being assertive before doing so in real life.

    b. Before your experiment(s), or on any day you're bothered by anxiety, shame, upset, rumination, or avoidance for at least an hour, use one or more of the reframing strategies. Use the reframing worksheets in the free tools.

c. Practice being a good parent to yourself after homework experiments and for any situation that triggers anxiety, shame, or rumination. Optionally, you may use the Being a Good Parent to Yourself Worksheet in the free tools.

CHAPTER 12

Rebelling and Acting as if: Using Experiments to Change Your Core Beliefs

In the last chapter, you identified your shame-based core beliefs and wrote first drafts of pride-based alternatives. I also discussed ways to affirm these new beliefs, through both proactive and reactive recitation, and by writing and reading core belief flash cards for your major anxiety trigger(s). In this chapter, I present a very powerful strategy of conducting experiments designed to rebel against your shame-based beliefs and act as if you fully embrace your pride-based beliefs.

Let's begin by discussing the progress you've been making through your self-therapy homework practice:

Describe how reciting your pride-based core beliefs with conviction—or listening to a recording or yourself doing so—has gone and felt for you. Are you doing so proactively (as a daily practice) and reactively (when you feel anxiety or shame)? How has your reaction changed during the course of the week? Have you modified these beliefs to make them resonate more?

_____

_____

_____

_____

How has it felt to read your flash card when your anxiety or shame have been triggered? Have you written additional flash cards for other triggers?

_____

_____

_____

Have you done paradoxical experiments, followed immediately by using head-held-high assertions (perhaps in addition to, or embedded within, straightforward experiments)? How has this strategy been going and feeling for you? What evidence have you gathered, and what have you learned?

_____

_____

_____

_____

In what ways has utilizing the Pride and Gratitude Log benefited you?

_____

_____

How well have you been able to maintain an external mindful focus whenever you're anxious?

_____

_____

Describe your use of any of these optional strategies, and in what ways they've been helpful. Are there certain ones you want to emphasize practicing more during the coming weeks in order to strengthen their effectiveness?

- Confident imagery
- Reframing
- Being a good parent to yourself

_____

_____

_____

_____

Remember, you're developing important strategies and skills that can benefit you for the rest of your life. There's no hurry. Take more time to do the homework practice if you need to before continuing with this chapter.

Using Experiments to Change Core Beliefs

From early on in your self-therapy work, you've been using experiments to test both your hot thoughts and your core beliefs. Each experiment has helped you gather evidence that counters your old shame-based attitudes about yourself and how you imagine others see you. In your Pride and Gratitude Log, you've also been gathering evidence to help you notice and appreciate your positive qualities.

Even with all the progress you've made, it's still only natural to continue having difficulty at times letting go of these old shame-based attitudes about yourself and fully embracing your newer pride-based beliefs. After all, the old attitudes are stored physically in neural pathways in your brain. Despite all your progress, there's no delete button in your brain to simply remove these old, unhealthy beliefs you've practiced for most of your life. Occasionally your old buttons will get pushed by experiences in the present, and the old beliefs will get triggered, along with the anxiety and shame they generate.

You can rev up the process of changing your core beliefs and building self-confidence by conducting experiments in which you defiantly **rebel** against your shame-based beliefs, and boldly **act as if** you fully embrace your pride-based beliefs. Here's how:

Rebel Experiments: Defying Your Shame-Based Core Beliefs

First identify the behavioral rules (the dos and don'ts) dictated by your shame-based beliefs. Then do a series of social anxiety experiments in which you deliberately and defiantly break these rules and do the opposite. *Rebel against the oppressive authority of your shame-based beliefs:* a personal form of civil disobedience to weaken their power over you. Disobey and defy your old core beliefs by doing the opposite of what they tell you to do, and see what you learn as a result!

For example, say your shame-based belief tells you that you're fundamentally deficient, so it sets the rule that you should avoid or minimize interacting with people you don't know well lest they discover your deficiencies and you get hurt. Dare to defy and rebel against that oppressive authority by conducting a series of experiments in which you initiate and extend conversations with whomever you damn well please! And if one person seems uninterested, view it as *their* loss, and initiate conversation with someone else instead!

In addition to doing straightforward experiments to rebel against your shame-based core beliefs, you can also conduct paradoxical experiments to defy their oppressive authority over you. This is similar to what we practiced in chapter 9, but it takes you a level deeper by targeting your underlying beliefs. For example, if your shame-based beliefs tell you to hide your imperfections lest others judge you as not good enough to like or respect, then defiantly choose to make a mistake, or ask a stupid question, or reveal your anxious symptoms when interacting with someone or speaking in a group. Then see what happens. Most of the time no one will even notice. If they do notice, their behavior toward you will likely not change and the interaction will go on as normal, indicating that they don't care. In the very unlikely event someone does react negatively to you, then use your head-held-high assertion and say, for example, "Oops. I guess we all say silly things from time to time, don't we!" Or "Yes, I sometimes do get a bit nervous talking to new people, but I'm enjoying our conversation." Then continue speaking as though nothing negative has occurred, and see what happens. You'll likely find that this was just a little blip, and it doesn't impact the conversation or the relationship at all. In the worst-case scenario, if the person does react very badly toward you, remind yourself that this simply means that they aren't a good match for you. Then defiantly move on to talk to someone else.

Act-As-If Experiments: Choosing to Live with Pride and Self-Confidence

Identify social anxiety experiments you want to conduct to help you make further progress toward your self-therapy goals. Then read your pride-based beliefs and ask yourself: "How would I act in this situation if I embraced these new core beliefs completely?" Then *act as if you fully embrace these pride-based beliefs* during the experiment, and see what you learn as a result!

For example, say you choose as an experiment to attend a social activity to work on your goal of making friends or dating. Perhaps your new core belief says that you have strengths and weaknesses like everyone else, and that if somebody doesn't like you, that just means they aren't a good match for you. Asking yourself how you would act if you fully embraced that pride-based belief, you decide to approach anybody you feel like talking to at the social activity. And, if you don't connect well with one person, you simply think, *Oh well, we just didn't click*, and then move on to talk to somebody else! No self-doubt or self-criticism. Just brush it off and continue socializing.

Similarly, in addition to doing straightforward experiments, you can also conduct paradoxical experiments in which you are acting as if you fully embrace your pride-based beliefs. For example, consider having conversations in which you nonchalantly mention some of your deficiencies without apology, or maybe use humor to tell funny stories of how you blundered and embarrassed yourself in front of others. Then see what happens. In this paradoxical approach, you're acting as if you fully embrace your pride-based belief that you have strengths and weaknesses like everyone else, and if somebody doesn't like you, that's *their* loss!

Which Approach to Use

Rebel experiments and act-as-if experiments are two sides of one coin. You'll generally end up working on similar experiments regardless of which strategy you choose.

Some people find it more motivating and empowering to evoke their rebellious spirit and defy their shame-based core beliefs. Others are dreamers and feel more motivated and empowered by boldly choosing to live in accordance with their pride-based beliefs. Many people find it helpful to use both approaches, depending on the experiment or their mood. You may even prefer to use both approaches simultaneously in a single experiment—both defying your shame-based beliefs and acting as if you fully embrace your pride-based beliefs—to increase your motivation to act with bold determination and self-confidence.

The following exercise will prepare you to use these two approaches to core belief change experiments in the coming weeks. First, closely read the example Core Belief Action Plan that follows, as this will give you many examples to incorporate into your own plan.

Core Belief Action Plan
(Example)

Your shame-based core beliefs:

I'm fundamentally deficient.

If someone sees any of my deficiencies, they won't respect or like me.

Your pride-based core beliefs:

I have strengths and weaknesses, just like everyone else.

People respect and like me for who I am and don't expect me to be perfect, just as I value others despite their imperfections.

Rules (dos and don'ts) dictated by your shame-based beliefs:

Don't go to social activities unless good friends will be there whom I can hang out with.

Don't initiate conversations with strangers, especially those I'm attracted to.

Don't join group conversations, or stay quiet when I am in groups.

Do script to make sure I have things to say.

Do avert eye contact and speak softly and briefly.

Do monitor my anxiety symptoms and try to hide them.

Do ask lots of questions to keep the focus on the other person.

Don't talk about myself, tell stories, or assert myself.

Do end conversations early to escape discomfort and avoid embarrassment.

Don't speak up at meetings, or keep it very brief if I have to speak.

Do use fast-acting drugs (alcohol, CBD, benzos, beta blockers) to hide my symptoms.

If you fully embraced your pride-based beliefs and lived your life accordingly, what would you do differently? (Be specific.)

> I'd go to any social activity I'm interested in, regardless of how many people I expect to know there.
>
> I'd try to initiate conversation with anyone I felt like talking to, including people I find attractive.
>
> I'd try to join and participate actively in any group conversation that I'm interested in.
>
> During any conversation, I'd say what pops into mind naturally without scripting it first.
>
> I'd make lots of eye contact, talk louder, and elaborate for a few sentences.
>
> I'd treat my anxiety symptoms like unimportant background noise, and keep my attention on the conversation and the people.
>
> I'd balance asking questions with speaking more about myself.
>
> I'd tell stories during conversations.
>
> I'd assert myself and honestly express my own opinions and feelings.
>
> I'd extend conversations longer whenever possible to see how well we connect and how much I enjoy it over time.
>
> I'd speak up at meetings whenever an idea enters my mind and there's an opportunity.
>
> During any interaction, I'd accept my anxiety as safe and temporary, and not drink or take other fast-acting drugs to try to quash it.

Your self-therapy goals you want to focus on now (objective/external and subjective/internal):

> Meet new people and invite them out socially.
>
> Make friends.
>
> Date people I'm attracted to.
>
> Give reports and presentations in meetings.

Experiments (straightforward and/or paradoxical) you plan to conduct to work on your goals in which you rebel against your shame-based beliefs (by breaking their rules) and/or act-as-if you fully embrace your pride-based beliefs:

Attend a group social activity weekly: initiate conversations with strangers (especially those I'm attracted to) and join group conversations.

Invite and go out with new people as friends or on dates.

In these conversations: no alcohol/meds, focus mindfully, treat anxiety symptoms as background noise, reveal more about myself, elaborate when I speak, tell stories, make more eye contact, speak louder, extend conversations longer.

(Paradoxical) During some conversations, show anxiety symptoms or say something stupid, then use a head-held-high assertion and continue conversing.

Speak up more often and longer at staff meetings (without taking meds).

Give a presentation at work or Toastmasters (without meds).

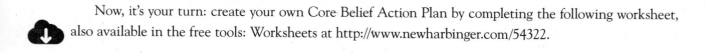

Now, it's your turn: create your own Core Belief Action Plan by completing the following worksheet, also available in the free tools: Worksheets at http://www.newharbinger.com/54322.

Core Belief Action Plan

Your shame-based core beliefs:

_____

_____

_____

_____

Your pride-based core beliefs:

_____

_____

_____

_____

Rules (dos and don'ts) dictated by your shame-based beliefs:

_____

_____

_____

_____

_____

_____

_____

If you fully embraced your pride-based beliefs and lived your life accordingly, what would you do differently? (Be specific.)

___

___

___

___

___

___

___

Your self-therapy goals you want to focus on now (objective/external and subjective/internal):

___

___

___

___

Experiments (straightforward and/or paradoxical) you plan to conduct to work on your goals in which you rebel against your shame-based beliefs (by breaking their rules), and/or act-as-if you fully embrace your pride-based beliefs:

How to Conduct Core Belief Change Experiments

Now that you've developed your personalized Core Belief Action Plan, how do you go about conducting the experiments you've chosen? Here are the steps:

1. Before your rebel or act-as-if experiment, complete the first portion of an *Experiment Worksheet*.

2. You may find it helpful to practice *confident imagery* before conducting your core belief change experiment. Start by reading your pride-based core beliefs. Then create vivid imagery—in mental pictures or verbal narration—of you doing the experiment while acting as if you fully embrace your pride-based beliefs, or boldly rebelling against your shame-based beliefs. Repeat the imagery multiple times until you feel less anxious and more self-confident doing the experiment. Try using imagery of different versions of your experiments: with the other people reacting to you in different ways, some negatively. Practice responding to any fears coming true in your imagery with confidence, making *head-held-high assertions*. Then conduct the experiment in real life!

3. During the experiment, remember to *focus mindfully* (externally, with curiosity) while treating your thoughts and feelings like background noise. And do your best to carry out the action steps you've chosen for that experiment. If you're doing a paradoxical experiment, couple it with *making your head-held-high assertion with a confident tone right after carrying out your paradoxical action*.

4. After your experiment, complete the final portion of the *Experiment Worksheet* to help you identify the evidence you gathered and the things you learned that will further strengthen your pride-based beliefs and weaken your shame-based attitudes. Remember to *be a good parent to yourself*. Affirm yourself for the positive action steps you've taken and the learning you've experienced. Don't beat yourself up or ruminate about imperfections, as that results in distress and shame. Instead, pat yourself on your back for the progress you've made, and identify what you want to do next time to make further progress.

5. Finally, continue making entries into your daily *Pride and Gratitude Log*, including examples that stem from your core belief change experiments. These rebel and act-as-if experiments generate evidence of your positive qualities and evidence that confirms your pride-based beliefs and refutes your shame-based beliefs. Your old core beliefs have created a negativity bias for most of your life in which you magnify your deficiencies and minimize—or don't even notice—your positive experiences and qualities. Record the positive evidence from your experiments and other experiences into your log, and remember to also write your underlying qualities these exemplify. Reread these entries whenever you want a confidence boost.

Self-Therapy Homework Practice

Visit http://www.newharbinger.com/54322 to download the worksheets for this chapter.

1. Choose and carry out one or more *rebel* or *act-as-if* experiments from your Core Belief Action Plan. Follow the five steps described in the previous section. Optionally, you may practice using confident imagery before your experiment. If you're doing a paradoxical experiment, couple it with making your head-held-high assertion with a confident tone right after carrying out your paradoxical action (both in imagery and in the real-life experiment). Use the Experiment Worksheet in the free tools before and after your experiment(s).

2. Continue making daily entries in your Pride and Gratitude Log, including evidence gathered from your core belief change experiments, and your underlying qualities your entries exemplify.

3. Affirming pride-based core beliefs:

    a. At least once daily, recite your pride-based core beliefs out loud with a tone of conviction, or listen to your recording. Do so proactively at a routine time, ideally early every day, so that it's fresh in your mind throughout the day. Also do so reactively whenever you're alone and feeling social anxiety or shame and perhaps ruminating. Then focus mindfully on a valued activity. Optionally, you may make changes in your pride-based belief to make them resonate more.

    b. Read your flash card, ideally out loud, whenever you anticipate experiencing the triggering situation. Optionally, you may write additional flash cards on other triggers and put these on your phone to read as needed.

4. Continue to practice having an external, mindful focus during your homework experiments and whenever you feel anxious around others.

5. [OPTIONAL] Practice any of the following strategies that you find helpful or that you haven't tried enough to determine how helpful it is.

    a. Practice confident imagery of conducting your experiment and being assertive before doing so in real life.

    b. Before your experiment(s), or on any day you're bothered by anxiety, shame, upset, rumination or avoidance for an hour or more, use one or more of the reframing strategies. Use the reframing worksheets in the free tools.

    c. Practice being a good parent to yourself after homework experiments, and for any situation that triggers anxiety, shame or rumination. Optionally use the Being a Good Parent to Yourself Worksheet in the free tools.

CHAPTER 13

That Was Then, This Is Now: Learning to Let Go of the Past

You created a Core Belief Action Plan in the last chapter in which you identified experiments designed to rebel against the dictates of your shame-based core beliefs, or act as if you fully embrace your pride-based beliefs. Both types of experiments are aimed at generating evidence to weaken the hold your old core beliefs have over you, which has resulted in so much social anxiety, shame, and life dissatisfaction. In this chapter, we'll discuss and practice a few additional CBT strategies aimed at helping you to further let go of your shame-based beliefs and to build pride and self-confidence.

Let's first explore your experience and progress in practicing the self-therapy homework:

What rebel or act-as-if experiments have you done? Did confident imagery help you build courage and motivation to carry out these experiments? Did any of your fears come true in conducting these experiments, whether straightforward or paradoxical? If so, were you able to respond to them using your head-held-high assertion? Most importantly, what evidence have you gathered through your experiments refuting your shame-based core beliefs and affirming your pride-based beliefs?

_____

_____

_____

_____

_____

_____

_____

_____

_____

In what ways has utilizing the Pride and Gratitude Log benefited you? Are you including evidence you've gathered through your rebel and act-as-if experiments?

_____

_____

_____

How has reciting your pride-based core beliefs with conviction—or listening to a recording or yourself doing so—been going and feeling for you? How has it felt to read your flash card when your anxiety or shame has been triggered? Have you modified your new core beliefs to make them resonate more, or written new flash cards on other triggers?

_____

_____

_____

_____

_____

_____

How well have you been able to maintain an external mindful focus whenever you're anxious?

_____

_____

In what ways have any of the following optional strategies been helpful for you? Are there certain ones you want to prioritize practicing in the coming weeks in order to strengthen their effectiveness?

- Confident imagery
- Reframing
- Being a good parent to yourself

_____

_____

_____

_____

Remember to not slip into the embrace of perfectionism here, which would only make you feel discouraged and unmotivated. You're developing important strategies and skills that can benefit you for the rest of your life. You don't need to rush it. Take more time to do the homework practice from the last chapter if you need to before continuing with this chapter.

Then vs. Now: Breaking the Link of Painful Memories

One reason why it's challenging to let go of your shame-based core beliefs is that they're embedded in powerful images or impressions in your mind that are based on painful memories of past experiences that recur when you're anxious in present situations. In other words, *you tend to see the present through the lens of the past in ways that distort your perceptions of what is actually happening in the here and now*…resulting in hot thoughts, safety-seeing behaviors, social anxiety, and shame. The common saying "it pushed my buttons" expresses this phenomenon: a present-day situation triggers old images, impressions, and feelings created by painful past experiences, which distort how you think, feel, and behave in the present.

An important CBT strategy called Then vs. Now (aka "stimulus discrimination training," Clark 2023b) will help you break this link between painful memories and present experiences. Practicing Then vs. Now, especially when conducting rebel or act-as-if experiments, will help you further reject your shame-based core beliefs and build self-confidence and pride.

This strategy begins by identifying the *images or impressions* that come to mind whenever you experience strong social anxiety. Close your eyes and imagine yourself in a present-day situation in which you're very socially anxious. You're not practicing confident imagery now. To the contrary, you're exploring what images or impressions come to mind when you're quite socially anxious. If you don't think much in pictures, describe your impression or feeling of how you come across and how others respond to you. Do this for just a minute or two, then open your eyes.

Describe in detail what image or impression you have about how you come across and how others respond:

_____
_____
_____
_____
_____

What's the worst thing about this image or impression? What does it mean to you? What shame-based old core belief does it evoke?

_____
_____
_____
_____

Now, reflect on the earliest time you can recall feeling this way. It's okay if you're not sure it's your very first such memory, or if your memory is actually a conglomerate of multiple similar experiences you've had. Now close your eyes for a minute or two, and recall what you experienced then, including how you felt, how you believe you came across, and how others reacted. It doesn't matter whether your memory is like a video or more of a verbal narrative. After a minute or two, open your eyes.

Describe your early social anxiety memory below: what happened, how you felt, how you believe you came across, and how others reacted:

_____
_____
_____
_____
_____

I congratulate you for having the courage to go into these painful places. It's for a good cause: learning to break the link between painful memories and your present experiences. This allows you to see and respond in the present for what is actually happening, as opposed to what you experienced so long ago. Have you noticed how similar your painful memory is to your present-day images or impressions when you're socially anxious? Do you see how these memories and images evoke your shame-based core beliefs?

Let's now look at the real-world evidence of how things are different then vs. now:

How old were you in your early memory, and how old are you now?

_____

Who were the people you were interacting with then, and how old were they? Who are you interacting with now when you're anxious, and how old are they?

_____

What was your occupation or role in life then? What is it now?

_____

How did people react to you in your early painful memory? How have people reacted to you when conducting your many homework experiments during this program?

_____

_____

_____

_____

How did you behave and come across then in your early memory? How have you behaved and come across in your present-day homework experiments?

_____

_____

_____

_____

Notice how the painful memories color your perceptions and feelings in present-day anxiety-triggering situations. When your old buttons (neural pathways) are pushed, you see the present through the lens of the past, triggering a vicious cycle of hot thoughts, safety-seeking behaviors, anxiety, and shame. But when you look at the evidence, you can see that things are very different for you now vs. then, especially when you focus mindfully, don't avoid, and drop other safety-seeking behaviors.

To further weaken the bond of your painful memories and the shame-based core beliefs they embed, *make it a goal in all your upcoming homework experiments and other anxiety-triggering situations to focus externally and notice how things are different now vs. then.* Afterward, record this evidence in your Pride and Gratitude Log.

Advantages vs. Disadvantages: Cost-Benefit Analysis of Core Beliefs

The impact of painful memories is only one reason why it's challenging to let go of your shame-based core beliefs. Another reason is that these old attitudes have helped you in some ways, especially in the past. They acted like your guide and protector throughout your younger years. Your old core beliefs are more like overprotective parents than evil forces that possess you. Still, however well-meaning, they make you suffer and hold your life back! It's hard to let go of an old helper, even one that's caused you so much pain and dissatisfaction. It's helpful to explore and understand the short-term benefits of your shame-based beliefs and their much greater longer-term costs, as well as the short-term costs of your pride-based beliefs, and their much greater longer-term benefits.

Before completing the following Advantages vs. Disadvantages Worksheet, I suggest you first review the completed example which follows. Then conduct your own cost-benefit analysis by completing the blank worksheet that follows (also available at http://www.newharbinger.com/54322).

Advantages vs. Disadvantages Worksheet
(Example)

Brief summary of your shame-based old core beliefs:

I'm different and don't fit in. I have poor social skills. If I don't meet other's expectations completely, they won't like or respect me. I should never hurt other people's feelings. Rejection mean I'm not good enough. If I appear or act anxious, people will think I'm weird, weak, or incompetent.

List the advantages of your old core beliefs. Consider the ways they've protected you, guided you, provided you with excuses to not try, and given you a sense of identity. Include advantages that were true in the past, even if they no longer work for you.

- They sometimes motivate me to try really hard to improve myself and excel at what I do.
- When I do well, I sometimes get praise and respect from others, which feels really good.
- I tend to avoid taking risks, which is easier and feels safer.
- This is how I'm used to seeing myself and my life; it feels familiar and secure.
- When I'm unhappy, I get to feel sorry for myself, which is somewhat comforting.

List the disadvantages of your old core beliefs. How have they hurt the way you feel, think, and behave? What impact have they had on your socializing, friendships, romantic relationships, recreation, hobbies, and career?

- They often lead me to procrastinate or avoid when I'm concerned I won't do well enough.
- They often cause me to worry and feel anxious about upcoming tasks and social activities.
- They often lead me to ruminate, and feel ashamed and depressed when I don't think I've met expectations, or when I'm rejected.
- I don't get to enjoy myself often because I'm so self-conscious.
- It's hard to meet people and make friends.
- I often withdraw from relationships rather than assert myself.
- I'm afraid to let people get very close to me, assuming they'll inevitably be disappointed in me.

- I don't develop new interests because I'm afraid I won't perform well enough.
- I often don't feel happy because I focus mainly on my failings.
- I miss out on a lot of opportunities because I feel discouraged or afraid to take risks.
- Life feels like a one struggle after another!

Review the advantages and disadvantages you've recorded and assign them each a percentage, totaling 100, to measure their relative strength and importance in your life:

Advantages of old shame-based core beliefs: 35%

Disadvantages of old shame-based core beliefs: 65%

Summary of your PRIDE-BASED NEW CORE BELIEFS:

I have commonalities and differences with everyone, as do all people. I converse and connect well with most people so long as I focus mindfully. People like and respect me for who I am, flaws and all. My feelings are as important as anyone's. Rejection just means the other person has different preferences or circumstances. It says nothing about my worth. Most people don't notice or care about my anxiety. I don't have to be perfect. Just be myself; that's good enough.

List the advantages of your new core beliefs. Consider how fully embracing them and living in accordance with them impacts how you feel and think and how different aspects of your life go. Include benefits you've already experienced as well as those you expect to experience as you continue living in accordance with your new beliefs:

- I'll procrastinate and avoid things less.
- I'll be less worried and anxious.
- I won't feel ashamed and depressed, and will ruminate a lot less.
- I'll enjoy myself more.
- It'll be easier and more fun meeting people and making friends.
- Relationships will probably go better for me since it'll be easier to assert myself, and I won't be so afraid of letting someone get close to me.
- I'll be able to develop new interests more easily.

- My life will feel fuller.
- I'll feel happier more often.
- I can still try to improve myself and excel, but not so desperately as before.
- It'll still feel good to get praise and respect from others, but it'll be less upsetting when I don't.
- It'll probably hurt a lot less when others reject me because I'll feel a lot better about myself and I won't take it personally.
- Although it may be challenging and feel unnatural at first, this new self-identity and lifestyle will probably get easier with time.

List the disadvantages of your new core beliefs. In what ways do they make things harder or scarier for you, at least in the short run? What negative consequences might they bring about, and how might you better deal with these consequences? (For example, taking more social risks might lead to more rejections and other disappointments. But not taking these personally—in accordance with your new core beliefs—will make it much less painful for you than you experienced in the mindset of your old beliefs, where you viewed them as signs of personal deficiency.)

- I may feel less motivated to try hard to improve myself and to excel.
- I may not get as much praise and respect from others for excelling.
- I will be taking risks a lot more often, which seems very scary and threatening.
- I'll be rejected more often if I socialize more and let people get closer to me. But it'll hurt a lot less because I feel better about myself and don't take it personally.
- It's going to be very hard and will feel unnatural to try to change my self-identity and lifestyle after growing so used to the old ways, but it'll get easier with practice.

Review the advantages and disadvantages you've listed of your new core beliefs and assign them each a percentage, totaling 100, to measure their relative strength and importance in your life:

Advantages of new pride-based core beliefs: 75%

Disadvantages of new pride-based core beliefs: 25%

Advantages vs. Disadvantages Worksheet

Brief summary of your shame-based old core beliefs:

_____

_____

_____

List the advantages of your old core beliefs. Consider the ways they've protected you, guided you, provided you with excuses to not try, and given you a sense of identity. Include advantages that were true in the past, even if they no longer work for you.

_____

_____

_____

_____

List the disadvantages of your old core beliefs. How have they hurt the way you feel, think, and behave? What impact have they had on your socializing, friendships, romantic relationships, recreation, hobbies, and career?

_____

_____

_____

_____

_____

Review the advantages and disadvantages you've recorded and assign them each a percentage, totaling 100, to measure their relative strength and importance in your life:

Advantages of shame-based old core beliefs: _____%

Disadvantages of shame-based old core beliefs: _____ %

Summary of your pride-based new core beliefs:

_____

_____

_____

_____

List the advantages of your new core beliefs. Consider how fully embracing them and living in accordance with them impacts how you feel and think and how different aspects of your life go. Include benefits you've already experienced as well as those you expect to experience as you continue living in accordance with your new beliefs:

_____

_____

_____

_____

_____

_____

_____

List the disadvantages of your new core beliefs. In what ways do they make things harder or scarier for you, at least in the short run? What negative consequences might they bring about, and how might you better deal with these consequences? (For example, taking more social risks might lead to more rejections and other disappointments. But not taking these personally—in accordance with your new core beliefs—will make it much less painful for you than you experienced in the mindset of your old beliefs, where you viewed them as signs of personal deficiency.)

___

___

___

___

Review the advantages and disadvantages you've listed of your new core beliefs and assign them each a percentage, totaling 100, to measure their relative strength and importance in your life:

Advantages of pride-based new core beliefs: _____%

Disadvantages of pride-based new core beliefs: _____%

Having completed this cost-benefit analysis of your old vs. new core beliefs, what are the key learning points you want to keep in mind when you experience social anxiety or shame or are tempted to avoid something due to fears?

___

___

___

___

___

___

Saying Goodbye: Letter Writing to Help You Let Go

Are there some people in your past from whom you've learned your shame-based core beliefs? Maybe it was specific things they told you, or examples they gave you, or painful experiences they caused you, that helped to create and shape these old mindsets. You cannot change anything that occurred in the past, of course. But you can change the self-defeating lessons that you've learned from the past. The letter-writing exercise that follows is designed to help you let go of these painful experiences and the old core beliefs they instilled. This is an optional exercise to do if you feel the need to gain further distance from the harmful impact of certain relationships.

Briefly list the key people and experiences that helped you to learn your shame-based core beliefs:

_____

_____

_____

_____

Now, write one or more letters to those who helped teach you these old core beliefs. Address three things in the letter(s):

1. what you have learned from them,

2. how these lessons have affected you at different points in your life, and

3. what you need to learn and do to overcome their negative influence on your life.

Express yourself with strong feeling. Don't hold yourself back. Don't edit or censor or be diplomatic. (Worry not; you won't send these letters!) Don't forget to include the third point about what you need to learn and do differently in order to move forward. This is a letter about taking personal responsibility, not just blaming.

Consider adding an optional fourth section in your letter in which you express forgiveness. Forgiveness doesn't have to mean exonerating, pardoning, or even understanding the person and what they did to you. Forgiveness can simply mean letting go of resentment and anger you bear toward them and moving on. Forgiveness is something you do for yourself as much as—or more than—for the person you forgive.

Save and reread the letter periodically. Write additional letters as the need arises. If you feel the desire to actually send such a letter, hold onto it for at least a few days. Consider what the consequences may be of sending the letter. Consider whether you wish to edit it in a way that might be better understood and received by the recipient.

Before writing your own letter(s), you may wish to read one that was written by a former client of mine who generously gave me permission to share it anonymously with others. You'll find this letter in the online bonus supplement for this chapter: http://www.newharbinger.com/54322.

Core Belief Arguments

Do you feel the need to strengthen your resolve in rejecting your old shame-based beliefs and embracing your new pride-based beliefs? You may want to try this optional exercise of conducting an argument with your old core beliefs, in writing or in role-play. Your objective in this exercise is to vanquish the old beliefs and banish them to the background so you can treat them like unimportant noise.

Written Argument

Write an argument between your shame-based core beliefs and yourself acting as if you fully embrace your pride-based beliefs. In your argument, use a combination of **reason** (the evidence that these old attitudes are inaccurate and have been harmful to you) and **strong emotion** (expressing yourself with passion, confidence, and perhaps anger or derision). Include some of the key points you noted in your Advantages vs. Disadvantages Worksheet (above). Make sure you don't get on the defensive in this argument or write it as a dry debate. Instead, take the offensive and inject passion and oomph into what you say, as doing so will likely feel more empowering and invigorating. You may find it helpful to periodically reread this argument and to add any additional points as you think of them.

Before writing your own core belief argument, I suggest you read two that were written by former clients of mine who generously granted permission to share them anonymously with others. They are in the online bonus supplement for this chapter: http://www.newharbinger.com/54322.

Role-Played Argument

If you're seeing a therapist, or have a trusted friend, try role-playing an argument in which the other person portrays your shame-based core beliefs. As in the written argument, you're portraying yourself acting as if you fully embrace your pride-based core beliefs. Remember to assert yourself with a combination of reason and strong emotion. Go for it with passion and oomph! Act as if you're sick and tired of your old beliefs and how they've impacted your life. Keep the argument going until you really feel empowered and invigorated. Before conducting your own argument, I suggest that you and your therapist or friend watch the clinical demonstration video I made about doing this type of role-play, linked in the free tools: Resources at http://www.newharbinger.com/54322.

Self-Therapy Homework Practice

Visit http://www.newharbinger.com/54322 to download the worksheets and other materials for this chapter.

NOTE: I suggest spending a couple weeks working on this final homework practice before moving on to the last chapter.

1. Choose and carry out two or more *rebel* or *act-as-if* experiments from your Core Belief Action Plan. Use the Experiment Worksheet in the free tools before and after your experiment(s).

    a. Optionally, you may practice using confident imagery before the experiment, including making head-held-high assertions to handle fears coming true.

    b. If you're doing a paradoxical experiment in real life, couple it with your head-held-high assertion, using a confident tone, right after carrying out your paradoxical action.

    c. When conducting your experiments—and during other anxiety-triggering interactions—focus externally and notice the ways things are different now vs. then (when your painful memory was formed). Record this evidence in your Pride and Gratitude Log.

2. Make daily entries in your Pride and Gratitude Log, including your underlying qualities they exemplify. Include positive evidence you gathered during experiments.

3. Affirming pride-based core beliefs:

    a. At least once daily, recite your pride-based core beliefs out loud with a tone of conviction, or listen to your recording. Do so proactively at a routine time, ideally early every day, so that it's fresh in your mind throughout the day. Also do so reactively whenever you're alone and feeling social anxiety or shame and perhaps ruminating. Then focus mindfully on a valued activity. Optionally, you may make changes in your pride-based beliefs to make them resonate more.

    b. Read your flash card, ideally out loud, whenever you anticipate experiencing the triggering situation. Optionally, you may write additional flash cards on other triggers and put these on your phone to read as needed.

4. Continue to practice having an external, mindful focus during your homework experiments and whenever you feel anxious around others.

5. [OPTIONAL] Following the instructions in this chapter, practice any of the following strategies that you find helpful, or that you haven't tried enough to determine how helpful it is.

a. Additional core belief change strategies:

- Reread and perhaps add to your Advantages vs. Disadvantages Worksheet.
- Write a letter to people who helped teach you your shame-based beliefs.
- Write or role-play a core belief argument.

b. Before your experiment(s), or on any day you're bothered by anxiety, shame, upset, rumination, or avoidance for at least an hour, use one or more of the reframing strategies. Use the reframing worksheets in the free tools.

c. Practice being a good parent to yourself after homework experiments and for any situation that triggers anxiety, shame, or rumination. Optionally, you may use the Being a Good Parent to Yourself Worksheet in the free tools.

CHAPTER 14

Continuing Forward: Making Progress on Your Own

You've been on quite a journey of self-therapy these past several months! You deserve to take pride in your many efforts, the courage and perseverance you've demonstrated by facing your fears, and the progress you've made in the process. Despite your inevitable imperfections—you *are* only human, after all!—it's important to pat yourself on the back rather than beat yourself up. This is how you'll further build pride and self-confidence and better position yourself to continue making progress on your own. So, this chapter begins by applying the being-a-good-parent-to-yourself strategy to discussing your experience in pursuing this self-therapy program. We'll then develop a plan for moving forward beyond this program: both to prevent relapse and to continue making further progress on your own.

Assessing Your Progress and Challenges

We'll be exploring your experience in this self-therapy program as a whole, in addition to in the last couple of weeks. So, before proceeding further, spend a few minutes glancing through all the worksheets and other exercises you've done throughout this program—both in the book itself and in items you printed out—to refresh your memory. Then proceed with answering the following questions. (The arrowed bullets signify CBT strategies and skills discussed in this program.)

- **Self-therapy goals:** Review the objective and subjective goals you wrote for yourself in chapter 1. Describe the ways you've made progress toward achieving each goal, even if you feel you have more progress to make.

  _____
  _____
  _____
  _____
  _____
  _____
  _____

- **External mindfulness and curiosity training:** Describe the progress you've made in focusing your attention externally and with curiosity whenever you're anxious, while treating any distracting thoughts and feelings as background noise. Describe your efforts in using your anxiety as a cue to get out of your head and into the moment: refocusing on the person, conversation, or activity with curiosity rather than judgment.

  _____
  _____
  _____
  _____
  _____
  _____

- **Behavioral experiments while dropping safety-seeking behaviors:**
  - Straightforward
  - Paradoxical
  - Surveys

- Rebel
- Act-as-if

You deserve a lot of credit for the courage and perseverance you've demonstrated in facing your fears by conducting many experiments throughout this program! Reviewing your experiment worksheets and your recollections, describe what you've been able to do that you previously avoided or that was harder for you before this program. Then summarize the key learning points you've achieved about your hot thoughts and core beliefs through these experiments. In what ways have you noticed differences *now* (how you are and how others react to you) *vs. then* (before working through this program)?

_____
_____
_____
_____
_____
_____
_____
_____
_____
_____
_____
_____
_____
_____
_____
_____

➤ **Being a good parent to yourself:** Describe how you've used this strategy and how it's benefitted you. Has it helped to lessen your rumination and negativity bias and build pride and self-confidence?

_____
_____
_____
_____

➤ **Reframing:** Which reframing strategies have you found most helpful? How have they benefited you, and for what circumstances do you find them most helpful?
   ➤ True-however-therefore
   ➤ Acceptance and problem solving
   ➤ The 3 Cs
   ➤ Very brief oral reframing
   ➤ In-depth reframing

_____
_____
_____
_____
_____

➤ **Confident imagery:** Describe how you've used this strategy and how it's benefitted you. Does it help motivate you to do things that you're anxious about, including challenging experiments? Does it help you build confidence about handling fears coming true?

_____
_____
_____
_____

> **Pride and Gratitude Log:** In what ways have you found this strategy to be beneficial? Has it helped improve your mood and self-confidence and lessen your negativity bias and rumination?

_____
_____
_____
_____
_____

> **Head-held-high assertion:** List times when you've used assertion in your experiments, whether to express your feelings or opinions or to stand up for yourself when a fear comes true. How has that felt and gone for you? Has this strategy—both in real life as well as in imagery and role-plays—helped you to build pride and self-confidence?

_____
_____
_____
_____
_____

> **Core belief change work:** Describe which of these core belief change strategies you've found helpful, and how they've benefited you. Which of your core beliefs have you had the most success in changing?

> > Reciting (or listening to your recording of) pride-based core beliefs

> > Writing and reading core belief flash cards

> > Conducting rebel or act-as-if experiments

> > Then vs. now: noticing how you and others are different from when your shame-based core beliefs first developed

> > Advantages vs. disadvantages: old vs. new core beliefs

> > Writing letters to those who helped teach you your old core beliefs

> > Core belief arguments: written or role-played

- **I am proud that:** Now it's time to pat yourself on the back! Remember, doing so will help you build pride and self-confidence and reduce shame and social anxiety. (Don't worry; we'll get to ways you can make further progress in the upcoming sections.) Reread all you've written above in this exercise. Then summarize below all the positive things you've done and the achievements you've made in this self-therapy program, no matter how imperfectly. Be specific. You deserve to take pride in all these!

- **Before and after scores for social anxiety and shame:** Now it's time for a numeric measure of your progress. Fill out the self-scoring social anxiety and shame questionnaires that you completed at the very start of this self-therapy program. Check the free tools: Resources at http://www.

newharbinger.com/54322 for links to these scales. Record your scores below in the AFTER section. Also copy your scores you recorded in chapter 1 in the BEFORE section. Optionally, to compute your percent improvement, subtract your after score from your before score; then divide that number by your before score; then multiply that answer by 100. For example, if your before score for total anxiety was 100, and your after score is 60, then your percent improvement is: (100–60) = 40 ÷ 100 = 0.4 X 100 = 40% improvement.

- **Leibowitz Social Anxiety Scale**

    BEFORE:

    anxiety score _____ avoidance score _____ total score _____ date _____

    AFTER:

    anxiety score _____ avoidance score _____ total score _____ date _____

    PERCENT IMPROVEMENT: _____%

- **External and Internal Shame Scale:**

    BEFORE: score_____ date_____

    AFTER: score_____ date_____

    PERCENT IMPROVEMENT: _____%

Maintaining and Furthering Your Progress

Cognitive behavioral therapy aims at helping you become your own therapist. Through this CBT self-therapy program, you've learned and practiced many strategies and skills that you can continue using on your own to guide you through the inevitable challenges that lie ahead, as well as help you further enhance your life satisfaction. There may well be times when you'll benefit from working with a cognitive behavioral therapist in the future. But by continuing to use the CBT strategies and skills you've learned here—both on a proactive, ongoing basis as well as reactively when you slip into an old pattern—you'll be in a much stronger position to prevent relapse and keep moving forward.

First, it's important to set realistic expectations: *lapses are inevitable, but relapse is preventable.* Lapses are slips into old patterns (e.g., moments of increased anxiety, shame, or hot thoughts; times you revert to avoidance, self-focused attention, or other safety-seeking behaviors); whereas a relapse is a prolonged return to old problems. Remember, old patterns are stored physically in neural pathways in your brain. Sometimes your old buttons will get pushed, and there's no delete key to get rid of these old neural pathways. But you can prevent a lapse from becoming a relapse by promptly using your CBT strategies and skills in reaction to any slip. Paradoxically, you can even turn lapses into opportunities not only to recover, but to make further progress!

Furthermore, making it a life priority to use CBT strategies and skills on a proactive, ongoing basis will not only prevent many lapses, but it will make you better prepared to respond to those lapses when they do occur, prevent relapse, and enhance your life by helping you make further progress toward your personal goals.

The Continuing Forward Worksheet that follows will serve as an important guide for you after completing this self-therapy program. Please read the following example worksheet, and notice how you relate, then take the time to thoughtfully complete the blank worksheet (also available at http://www.newharbinger.com/54322). This will serve as your guide to continue making progress on your own after this program and to prevent relapse. Please also review the list of CBT strategies and skills we've used in this program that are outlined in the many arrowed bullets earlier in this chapter. Include in your Continuing Forward Worksheet those strategies and skills you have found most helpful, and those you'd like to practice more.

Continuing Forward Worksheet
(Example)

Personal goals (objective and subjective) for the coming year or so:

- to make more friends and connect more with current friends
- to continue dating
- to speak up more often and longer in staff meetings
- to assert my opinions in groups and with friends
- to network and apply for jobs
- to minimize rumination
- to continue increasing my self-confidence and pride while reducing social anxiety and shame

Personal vulnerabilities and triggers to social anxiety and shame (situations, interactions, and experiences that often trigger your old core beliefs and hot thoughts). Be specific:

- mingling in large groups of strangers
- expressing romantic interest in someone
- speaking more vulnerably or positively about myself
- speaking longer in groups
- expressing my opinions when others may disagree
- criticizing myself in my thoughts for imperfections
- comparing my weaknesses with others' strengths

Signs of a slip/lapse (your typical hot thoughts and safety-seeking behaviors that signal you're slipping into unhelpful old patterns). Be specific:

- avoiding something because of anticipatory anxiety
- focusing internally during an interaction on scripting and self-criticism
- saying I agree when I actually disagree
- ruminating

Proactive CBT strategies and skills you plan to use on an ongoing basis to help you make progress toward your personal goals and prevent some lapses. Be specific about what you plan to do, and how often:

- Read this worksheet weekly during my first cup of coffee on Sundays.

- Plan and do two behavioral experiments to work on my goals every week: one at work, and one socially. Conduct these as act-as-if experiments to strengthen my pride-based core beliefs. Incorporate paradoxical goals and head-held-high assertions into one experiment each week.

- Practice using confident imagery when I have a lot of anticipatory anxiety about an experiment or other experience, or when planning a paradoxical experiment. Incorporate using a head-held-high assertion for fears coming true into the imagery.

- Practice external mindfulness during all experiments and whenever else I feel anxious.

- Recite new core beliefs daily.

- Read my core belief flash card whenever I feel anticipatory anxiety about that trigger.

- Keep writing in my Pride and Gratitude Log daily, including evidence I gather from experiments.

Reactive CBT strategies and skills you plan to use when you have slipped into old patterns. Be specific:

- Whenever I start to ruminate, use one of the short reframing strategies followed by focusing mindfully on an activity I value. If I continue to ruminate for an hour, then complete an in-depth reframing worksheet, followed by getting engrossed in a valued activity.

- Whenever I have avoided something due to anxiety, or relied on safety-seeking behaviors when feeling uncomfortable during an interaction, don't beat myself up! Instead, turn it into a learning experience by planning and doing a behavioral experiment to work on the same challenge in the near future.

Continuing Forward Worksheet

Personal goals (objective and subjective) for the coming year or so:

_____
_____
_____
_____
_____
_____
_____

Personal vulnerabilities and triggers to social anxiety and shame (situations, interactions, and experiences that often trigger your old core beliefs and hot thoughts). Be specific:

_____
_____
_____
_____
_____
_____
_____

Signs of a slip/lapse (your typical hot thoughts and safety-seeking behaviors that signal you're slipping into unhelpful old patterns). Be specific:

_____

_____

_____

_____

_____

Proactive CBT strategies and skills you plan to use on an ongoing basis to help you make progress toward your personal goals and prevent some lapses. Be specific about what you plan to do, and how often:

_____

_____

_____

_____

_____

Reactive CBT strategies and skills you plan to use when you have slipped into old patterns. Be specific:

_____

_____

_____

_____

_____

_____

_____

Continuing Forward with Pride

You deserve to take pride in the good work you've done in this challenging self-therapy program! However imperfectly, you've demonstrated courage and perseverance in your efforts. You've made real progress in overcoming your social anxiety and shame, building your self-confidence and pride, and moving forward toward your personal goals. You've developed a set of evidence-based strategies and skills that—if you continue to use them proactively and reactively—will help you maintain the progress you've made, prevent relapse, and enhance your life by making more progress on your personal goals.

Do not let yourself slip into perfectionism, in which you disqualify the positive of what you've learned, done, and achieved by ruminating about the negative. Instead, be a good parent to yourself and affirm the positive steps you've taken. *Read your Continuing Forward Worksheet at least once every week as a regular reminder to utilize your CBT strategies proactively and reactively.* For a refresher, or to strengthen certain strategies and skills, reread certain chapters and work on the self-therapy homework suggested there. And don't hesitate to reach out for professional assistance from a cognitive behavioral therapist if you ever feel the need for further guidance and support. To obtain referral sources to CBT providers with expertise in helping people with social anxiety, use the link in the free tools: Resources at http://www.newharbinger.com/54322.

Congratulations for your good work, the courage and perseverance you've demonstrated, and all the progress you've made! I wish you all the best as you continue your life journey forward, with increasing self-confidence and pride.

References

Bruce S., K. Yonkers, M. Otto, J. Eisen, R. Weisberg, M. Pagano, M. Shea, and M. Keller. 2005. "Influence of Psychiatric Comorbidity on Recovery and Recurrence in Generalized Anxiety Disorder, Social Phobia, and Panic Disorder: A 12-Year Prospective Study." *American Journal of Psychiatry* 162: 1179–1187.

Burns, D. 1999. *Feeling Good: The New Mood Therapy*, rev. ed. New York: HarperCollins.

Canvin, L., M. Janecka, and D. Clark. 2016. "Focussing Attention on Oneself Increases the Perception of Being Observed by Others." *Journal of Experimental Psychopathology* 7: 160–171.

Clark, D. 2023a. "Decatastrophizing Behavioral Experiment-Adult & Adolescent" [Social Anxiety Disorder Training Videos]. OXCADAT Resources, Oxford University. https://oxcadatresources.com/social-anxiety-disorder-training-videos.

Clark, D. 2023b. "Stimulus Discrimination Training" [Social Anxiety Disorder Training Videos]. OXCADAT Resources, Oxford University. https://oxcadatresources.com/social-anxiety-disorder-training-videos.

de Ponti, N., M. Matbouriahi, P. Franco, M. Harrer, C. Miguel, D. Papola, A. Sicimoğlu, P. Cuijpers, and E. Karyotaki. 2024. "The Efficacy of Psychotherapy for Social Anxiety Disorder: A Systematic Review and Meta-analysis." *Journal of Anxiety Disorders* 104: 102881.

Ellis, A. 2016. *How to Control Your Anxiety Before It Controls You*. New York: Citadel Press.

Ginat-Frolich, R., E. Gilboa-Schechtman, J. Huppert, I. Aderka, L. Alden, Y. Bar-Haim, et al. 2024. "Vulnerabilities in Social Anxiety: Integrating Intra- and Interpersonal Perspectives." *Clinical Psychology Review* 109: 102415.

Hofmann, S. 2023. *CBT for Social Anxiety: Simple Skills for Overcoming Fear and Enjoying People*. Oakland, CA: New Harbinger Publications.

Hope, D., R. Heimberg, and C. Turk. 2019. *Managing Social Anxiety: A Cognitive behavioral Therapy Approach, Therapist Guide and Workbook*, 3rd ed. Oxford: Oxford University Press.

Koban, L., R. Schneider, Y. Ashar, J. Andrews-Hanna, L. Landy, D. Moscovitch, and J. Arch. 2017. "Social Anxiety Is Characterized by Biased Learning About Performance and the Self." *Emotion* 17: 1144–1155.

Liu, X., P. Yi, L. Ma, W. Liu, W. Deng, X. Yang, M. Liang, J. Luo, N. Li, and X. Li. 2021. "Mindfulness-Based Interventions for Social Anxiety Disorder: A Systematic Review and Meta-analysis." *Psychiatry Research* 300: 113935.

Mayo-Wilson, E., S. Dias, I. Mavranezouli, K. Kew, D. Clark, A. Ades, and S. Pilling. 2014. "Psychological and Pharmacological Interventions for Social Anxiety Disorder in Adults: A Systematic Review and Network Meta-analysis." *Lancet Psychiatry* 1: 368–76.

McEvoy, P. M., L. M. Saulsman, and R. M. Rapee. 2017. *Imagery-Enhanced CBT for Social Anxiety Disorder*. New York: Guilford Press.

National Institute of Mental Health. 2024. "Social Anxiety Disorder." https://www.nimh.nih.gov/health/statistics/social-anxiety-disorder.

Padesky, C. 1997. "A More Effective Treatment Focus for Social Phobia?" *International Cognitive Therapy* 11: 1–3.

Riccardi, C., K. Korte, and N. Schmidt. 2017. "False Safety Behavior Elimination Therapy: A Randomized Study of a Brief Individual Transdiagnostic Treatment for Anxiety Disorders." *Journal of Anxiety Disorders* 46: 35–45.

Larry Cohen, LICSW, A-CBT, is cofounder and chair of the National Social Anxiety Center (NSAC), an association of more than thirty regional clinics around the US dedicated to fostering evidence-based services to people struggling with social anxiety. He has directed the Social Anxiety Help clinic (NSAC District of Columbia) in Washington, DC, since 1990 where he has provided cognitive behavioral therapy (CBT) for more than 1,000 persons with social anxiety, and has conducted one hundred twenty-week social anxiety CBT groups. Cohen is certified as a diplomate in CBT by the Academy of Cognitive and Behavioral Therapies (ACBT), which has also conferred on him the status of fellow for having "made sustained outstanding contributions to the field of cognitive therapy."

Foreword writer **Richard Heimberg, PhD**, is an internationally recognized expert on CBT for social anxiety disorder (SAD). He is the Thaddeus L. Bolton Professor Emeritus in the department of psychology and neuroscience at Temple University, where he founded and directed a specialty social anxiety clinic, and he was previously professor in the department of psychology at the University at Albany of the State University of New York.

Real change *is* possible

For more than fifty years, New Harbinger has published proven-effective self-help books and pioneering workbooks to help readers of all ages and backgrounds improve mental health and well-being, and achieve lasting personal growth. In addition, our spirituality books offer profound guidance for deepening awareness and cultivating healing, self-discovery, and fulfillment.

Founded by psychologist Matthew McKay and Patrick Fanning, New Harbinger is proud to be an independent, employee-owned company. Our books reflect our core values of integrity, innovation, commitment, sustainability, compassion, and trust. Written by leaders in the field and recommended by therapists worldwide, New Harbinger books are practical, accessible, and provide real tools for real change.

MORE BOOKS from
NEW HARBINGER PUBLICATIONS

THE INNER CRITIC WORKBOOK

Self-Compassion and Mindfulness Skills to Reduce Feelings of Shame, Build Self-Worth, and Improve Your Life and Relationships

978-1648484292 / US $25.95

THE DIALECTICAL BEHAVIOR THERAPY SKILLS WORKBOOK FOR SHAME

Powerful DBT Skills to Cope with Painful Emotions and Move Beyond Shame

978-1684039616 / US $25.95

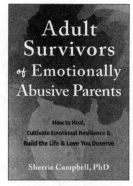

ADULT SURVIVORS OF EMOTIONALLY ABUSIVE PARENTS

How to Heal, Cultivate Emotional Resilience, and Build the Life and Love You Deserve

978-1648482632 / US $18.95

THE ADULT ADHD AND ANXIETY WORKBOOK

Cognitive Behavioral Therapy Skills to Manage Stress, Find Focus, and Reclaim Your Life

978-1648482434 / US $25.95

OVERCOMING IMPOSTER ANXIETY

Move Beyond Fear of Failure and Self-Doubt to Embrace Your Worthy, Capable Self

978-1648481086 / US $18.95

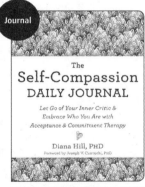

THE SELF-COMPASSION DAILY JOURNAL

Let Go of Your Inner Critic and Embrace Who You Are with Acceptance and Commitment Therapy

978-1648482496 / US $18.95

newharbingerpublications
1-800-748-6273 / newharbinger.com

(VISA, MC, AMEX / prices subject to change without notice)
Follow Us

Don't miss out on new books from New Harbinger.
Subscribe to our email list at **newharbinger.com/subscribe**

Did you know there are **free tools** you can download for this book?

Free tools are things like **worksheets**, **guided meditation exercises**, and **more** that will help you get the most out of your book.

You can download free tools for this book—whether you bought or borrowed it, in any format, from any source—from the New Harbinger website. All you need is a NewHarbinger.com account. Just use the URL provided in this book to view the free tools that are available for it. Then, click on the "download" button for the free tool you want, and follow the prompts that appear to log in to your NewHarbinger.com account and download the material.

You can also save the free tools for this book to your **Free Tools Library** so you can access them again anytime, just by logging in to your account! Just look for this button on the book's free tools page.

+ Save this to my free tools library

If you need help accessing or downloading free tools, visit **newharbinger.com/faq** or contact us at **customerservice@newharbinger.com**.